CONCILIUM

Religion in the Seventies

Concilium 111 (1/1978): Sociology of Religion

COMMUNICATION IN THE CHURCH

Edited by
Gregory Baum and
Andrew Greeley

A CROSSROAD BOOK
The Seabury Press · New York

1978
The Seabury Press
815 Second Avenue
New York, N.Y. 10017

Library of Congress Catalog Card Number: 78-65735
ISBN 0-8164-0369-4
ISBN: 0-8164-2170-6 (pbk.)
Printed in the United States of America

CONTENTS

Part III
Communication between the Hierarchy and Lower Levels

Part IV
Theory

Editorial

THE CHRISTIAN Church has always understood itself as a community, more precisely as a community of communities (*communitas communitatum*). Fellowship, interdependence, mutuality, exchange, communication—these belong to the substance of Christ's body on earth. In fact, the Christian Church has regarded itself as the sacrament of unity: that is to say, as the human community that reveals, anticipates and to some extent actualizes the community which the human family, divided by structures of sin, is destined to be in the age of God's kingdom. If we look at the universal Christian community, we should be able to read what the world community ought to be like, and what in fact it is appointed to be in God's providence. The Catholic Church, in particular, has claimed that the promises of God for the future reconciliation of the human race are visibly embodied in its own ecclesial unity.

The unity of the Church proclaimed in the ancient creeds is implicit in Christ's work of redemption, in the gifts of faith, hope and love, and in the sacraments of baptism and the eucharist. But the troubled passage from the implicit to the explicit is another story, a story we usually call church history. In this issue, we examine the communication between different sectors of the Catholic Church today, between public preaching and the faithful (I), between sectors of the Church situated in different national communities (II), and between bishops and lower levels (III.) Finally we offer theoretical reflections on what communication in the church ought to be (IV).

The present issue reveals—and this will not surprise the reader—that communication in the Catholic Church has been in varying degrees interrupted or distorted. The sacramental sign which the Church is meant to be is considerably obscured in world history. The Church's canonical structures, we note, are not simply more or less useful ecclesiastical arrangements that have evolved over the centuries, but have theological substance: they are meant to reveal the Church as the fellowship of believers, in communication with one another. To the extent that these structures fail to facilitate communication, they are actually counter-signs obscuring the credibility of the Gospel.

At the 1977 annual meeting of the editorial board of *Concilium,* held at the Catholic University of Notre Dame at South Bend, Indiana, USA, a three-day public exchange took place, involving the editor-theologians of *Concilium* and a group of American theologians and social scientists, on issues of great urgency for the Church today. During a public discussion following a presentation of the canonist Peter

Huizing on the requirements of canon law for today, a common question emerged that remained wholly unanswered. Why is it, the gathering wondered, that public meetings of canon lawyers, theologians, social scientists and well-informed believers without specialized training rapidly come to an agreement on the need for plural structures and institutional flexibility—whether these meetings are held in Europe, the Americas, Africa or Asia—whereas meetings involving the canonists of the Roman Curia come to such different conclusions? How can one explain such unanimity in the Catholic Church with such radical disagreement? It becomes increasingly necessary, therefore, to examine with the help of the social sciences the structures of communication in the Church in order to locate more clearly the points where conversation breaks down, authority encounters incomprehension, and communication is distorted; and thus where the visible community fails to give witness to its sacramental reality.

Gregory Baum

PART I

Preaching and the Reception of Doctrine

Reyes Mate

Currents of Opposition
in the Spanish Church

JOURNALISM and everyday conversation take for granted that the
Spanish Church is deeply divided: there is a Church of the 'crusade',
one of the *'aggiornamento'* and a third one 'of the people'.

Discounting the pretentious and abusive epithets hurled from one
side to the other, there is no denying that clearly defined currents are
ruffling the waters of the Church in Spain. They are more than spiritual
attitudes, since they have a definite ideological basis and a minimum of
institutional support. Only by recourse to history can this situation be
properly understood.

THE CHURCH OF THE 'CRUSADE'

In 1939, with the victory of the generals behind the 'coup' of 1936, a
model of the Church, which came to be known as *National Catholicism,* was imposed. It was made up of the following elements: *(a)* a
traditionalist inheritance deriving from the teachings of Donoso Cortés
and Balmes, consisting in condemnation of the European process of
political secularization, renunciation of modern rationalism and affirmation of religion as the principle of political legitimacy; *(b)* the ideology of 'social Catholicism', the flag of the Spanish laity, whose rejection of liberalism was equalled only to their zeal for turning the social
encyclicals into a rich man's charter; *(c)* Falangism, the Spanish version of National Socialism, which aimed at creating a New Spain in the
image of Imperial Spain, the Spain of the sword and the cross.

The result of this imposition was the establishment of a neo-baroque

3

Church, which literally obliged the country to get up at dawn with a rosary and go to bed beating its breast. This model of the Church lasted unchallenged from 1939 to 1953, years of autarchy and poverty, but its decline began immediately after this period for two main reasons. The first of these was the ending of the international blockade with the signing of the Concordat with the Holy See and the treaty of friendship with the United States (1953). This international opening began the slow economic take-off, which gathered momentum with the 'Stabilization Plan' of 1958 worked out by the technocrats of the Opus Dei. This economic development, though launched from the basis of totalitarian political theories, was powerless to hinder a corresponding development and reorganization of the working-class movement that had been strangled since the Civil War. The second reason was the self-imposed exile of the most respected Francoist intellectuals. The military coup had meant death or exile for the powerful *intelligentsia* of the Republic. Now, the few personalities of any note who accepted the Franco régime gradually lost heart in the face of its continued brutality. In 1949, Pedro Laín Entralgo published his polemical work *España como Problema* (Spain as a Problem); in 1953, Julian Marías published *El existencialismo en España* (Existentialism in Spain); in 1952, José-Luis López Aranguren published *Catolicismo y protestantismo como formas de existencia* (Catholicism and Protestantism as modes of existence). These thinkers undermined the philosophical and theological bases of National Catholicism: Christianity did not come to an end with the Middle Ages, nor can the State be organized like an Order of Knights Templar. So a new ecclesial movement was born, strongly influenced by French Catholicism; while calling for development of the Franco régime, it also campaigned for the institution of human rights.

THE CHURCH OF THE 'AGGIORNAMENTO': A CHURCH FOR DEMOCRACY

This movement, numerically in a minority and without any real weight in the episcopate at the time of Vatican II, felt its way of thinking confirmed by the teachings of the Council, and ended by embracing the majority of the Spanish bishops. In 1973, the Episcopal Conference produced a document on 'The Church and the political community', which established a model of the Church that remains in force today. This marked a break with National Catholicism, replacing it with 'mutual independence and healthy collaboration' between Church and State. This model of the Church supposes acceptance of the modern principle of the secular nature and the autonomy of the political sphere, while promising 'healthy collaboration' with a State that takes the democratic ideal underlying this modern concept of politics seriously.

Don Vicente Tarancón, Cardinal Archbishop of Madrid and President of the Bishops' Conference, defined this relationship between Church and State in his homily before King Juan Carlos on 27 November 1975: 'in exchange for such strict requirements (the democratic principle), the Church as energetically assures the obedience of citizens, to whom it teaches the moral duty of supporting the legitimate authority in all that is ordered to the common good'.

This Church admits a plurality of political options for Christians since it bases its concept of the Church on faith in Jesus Christ. This faith, divorced from historical contingency, allows a plurality of choice without this affecting the unity of the Church. Such an understanding of the Church, so like that in vogue in most European democracies, nonetheless has a special significance—which can escape from a cursory consideration—for the Church in Spain.

Recognition of the democratic principle, which in turn defines this new ecclesial model, is a *victory* for which many sectors of Spanish society have fought. But those who have put most into the struggle and who have paid most dearly for the victory are the workers' organizations and parties. This is a fact.

Part of the Church has been distinguished by its active presence in this struggle. The important part played by Christian militants in the reorganization of the workers' movement and the struggle against Francoism has not yet been documented, but no one has any doubts on the score of its extent and importance, so that a correct account of the evolution of Spanish society during the Franco era would be inconceivable without giving it its due. Such citizens, militants in Socialist and Communist organizations, and Christians as well, by their very existence present the true test of the calibre of the democracy to which the Church has promised its 'healthy collaboration'.

These class organizations include the strengthening of a liberal, bourgeois democracy as part of their political strategy, but of course without abandoning their long-term Socialist goals. But they are prepared for the road to lead by way of the majority wishes of the people.

This being the case, the attitude of the Church to these Marxist organizations is difficult to understand: they are placed beyond the limits of the plurality of choice in which the Christian can indulge. He cannot be a 'red' or vote for a Marxist party. This anti-Socialist belligerence of the official line reveals the political bias beneath its political 'neutrality', while at the same time excluding these Christian Socialists from the ranks of Christian orthodoxy.

The Church's adjustment to bourgeois democracy is not a casual one: there is a hidden connivance between the 'new' Church and a particular version of the principle of secularization that in no way contradicts the feudal marriage between throne and altar. The mark of the modern State is, in reality, the contradiction between its constitutional principles, inherited from the revolutionary ideals of 1789, and its social reality: a deeply divided society. This means that the State, instead of being the political embodiment of all the interests of its citizens, is an instrument at the service of its ruling class. This State—which is not, and cannot be, the representative embodiment of the aspirations of its citizens, since by failing to recognize social antagonism, it deprives its citizens of the material means of becoming true citizens: that is, equal and free—in effect constitutes itself a transcendental body requiring the sacrifice of specific individuality; in exchange, it receives the hollow accolade of being 'sovereign' or the 'principle of political legitimization'. Such a State, for all its laicism, bears a strong resemblance to a certain type of religious behaviour— that marked by sacrifice of the individual to divine transcendence, in exchange for the theological accolade of man being recognized as king of creation.

Both cases produce an isolated man, who can neither be a citizen nor become a neighbour, a miserable being who has condemned himself to his own misery through his acceptance of submission to a supreme body (God or the State), which exists thanks to his self-negation.

This convergence of the bourgeois State and *aggiornamento* religiosity transcends the formal sphere and extends to particular doctrines. So we find theological sanctioning of private property, the present model of family life, and other bourgeois concepts; or acceptance of private education, as opposed to the free, socialized system. As it affects Spain, this material convergence is summed up in the Church's claim to a monopoly of morality in the new State, since it sees itself as the faithful guardian of the natural order. Hence the Church's reluctance to become too identified with the Christian Democrats, who are only a fraction of the Centre, whereas the Church's interests coincide with those of a broad spectrum of the political Centre.

From this cosy standpoint, the new Spanish Church can afford not to be sparing with its compliments to 'political autonomy', since this is in fact defending a particular brand of politics. Nor should one be surprised by the use it makes of terms belonging to political theology. Any theology that puts its religious weight behind the 'eschatological reserve', a previous affirmation of secular autonomy, will be welcomed in Spain, since this autonomy functions as a sanction for the liberal State and the 'eschatological reserve' can act as a corrective function within its politics, but not as a criticism of its essentials. It is true that political theology—at least at its outset—saw the 'eschatological reserve' as conditioning secular praxis in a particular direction; the 'reserve' stems from the memory of Jesus of Nazareth; this memory, insofar as it anticipates the future of humanity, demands a praxis of liberation, to bring about the kingdom and salvation. So it favours revolutionary action. But when this 'reserve' is interpreted from a standpoint of ingenuous acceptance of secularization, the faith and the Church become mere accompanists of the ruling power.

The great achievement of this Church of the *aggiornamento* is to have marginalized the Church of the 'crusade'. This is now a minority Church, thinly represented among the bishops, although it still has considerable social influence, thanks to its implantation in the apparatus of the Franco State, which is still flourishing. The real service done to Christianity is the unmasking of the nature of this 'crusading' Church: as it loses the support of the bishops and its social hegemony, this Church stands revealed as a fundamentally political ecclesial structure. It is now the lackey of political groups of the extreme Right. It is not shy of criticizing and threatening the conciliar stance of the Vatican and the bishops. Its orthodoxy is its defence of the previous régime, the quintessence, it claims, of a model of Christian civilization outside which the Church loses its identity.

There are, in fact, two tendencies within this Church. On the one hand, the reactionary attitude of organizations like the 'Priestly Brotherhoods' and of the minority of the bishops, to which one has to add the violence of the 'Warriors of Christ the King', who have put themselves on a war footing against those who are attacking their model of Christian civilization. On the other, the subtle politics of the Opus Dei, which is using its immense economic power and social influence to combat the bishops' decision to respect the liberal principle of political autonomy.

Its view that the identity of the Church is endangered by the disappearance of the feudal model of Christian civilization is based on a particular apologetics, and a particular ecclesiology and Christology. If its adherents are prepared to renounce the official orthodoxy, this is because they value a certain model of civilization above everything else. This is why this Church still survives under the umbrella of extreme right-wing political organizations.

OUTLAWED CHRISTIANS

The Achilles' heel of the Church of the *aggiornamento* is the existence of Christian freedom fighters and Christian militants in outlawed organizations. The Church still maintains that there is a limit to Christian pluralism: militancy in Marxist socialism—that is, in 'atheist and materialist' organizations thereby opposed to the Christian faith—is outside this limit. This ecclesial judgment is a form of political judgment since it limits a Christian's field of possible choices; it is also a religious disqualification, in that it excludes Marxist socialism, which many Christians have now embraced as a specific form of culture, from the conditions under which a Christian existence is held to be possible.

The Church bases its attitude on a dual principle: first, that identity of faith consists in belonging to a single Church: the profane event can in no case be a theological *locus;* second, that the Christian faith cannot develop in certain cultural contexts: Marxist culture, for example, exhausts it, strangles it and destroys it.

These two principles are mutually exclusive. In effect, if identity of faith is abstracted from any historical context, then all historical contexts should be a matter of indifference to it; but if it is so sensitive to the Socialist context, it is because it knows from experience that it needs a particular context—and, furthermore, that it has already chosen one in liberal democracy.

The ecclesial stance adopted by these outlawed Christians starts precisely from their understanding of the contradiction inherent in the official model. Their theological logic goes like this: *first,* a religious evaluation of the historical event: the social and political process of liberating the oppressed is a *sign of the times* that not only announces, but also anticipates—and therefore *is*—the coming of the kingdom. One has to do away with the theological megalomania for which the terms 'kingdom' and 'salvation' refer only to an uncontaminated transcendence, or to cosmic omega-points. Jesus had no hesitation in referring to a passing cure of blindness as 'the coming of the kingdom', or in calling a generous gesture of Zaccheus' 'a coming of salvation'. The passing event is a theological event, and, therefore *also is* the advent of the kingdom and of salvation.

Second, the religious value of such signs is made present in the challenge the event poses to the Christian conscience. The Christian knows himself to be affected by that moment of general liberation, the fruit of so many historical sorrows. And Spanish Christians understand this challenge as recognition of the age-old inaction of their Church in relation to the liberation of the oppressed, and as a demand for solidarity with all those Christians who have been outlawed by the Church as a result of their adherence to the cause of the oppressed.

It is not a question of making a Manichean judgment—the good on this side, the bad on that—but of recognizing the constant ambiguity in which the Spanish Church has existed, and which appears to be continuing. So the challenge becomes a need for conversion: the Christian is not born a brother to others; active brotherhood, *being* a neighbour, is won through conversion: the natural reaction faced with the traveller attacked by a thousand forms of injustice is to pass by on the other side. If you want to be a Samaritan you have to make yourself do it.

Third, neighbourliness, or becoming a neighbour to the oppressed, has a logical incidence on political activity. *Neighbourliness* implies, in the short and medium term, the institutionalization of *citizenship,* that is, the solidarity inherent in living together in society. This means attacking a type of state and a type of society that is committing a serious fraud with its concept of citizenship: it legitimizes its form of state by an appeal to this quality, while in fact ignoring it and crushing it. If intersubjectivity is an essential definition, not to say the central definition, of the subject of faith, then this same faith is constituted in a historical presupposition that requires, here and now, the establishment of a society based on the sovereignty and solidarity of its members. A rich dialectical relationship between *neighbourliness* and *citizenship* is set up, pregnant with liberation.

THE THEOLOGICAL LOCUS 'WITHOUT THE WALLS'

The deep currents that are dividing the Spanish Church herald the demise of scientific theology, that is, of the pretensions of a theological theory, elaborated in the workshop of a Theological Institute, to universal validity. These workshops are in fact acting as research departments for a certain kind of Church. In this country we have found the evidence that the historical and political event is an authentic theological *locus.* Both the Church of the Crusade and the outlawed Christians know this and agree on it. The difference between them stems from the content: the former, by giving an absolute value to the established order, renounce the future and subordinate everything to maintenance of the *status quo.* These theo-politics are a political manipulation of religion. The latter, on the other hand, situate themselves inside the historical event which takes freedom and the future as its substance, and is therefore a process of liberation.

Such a Christian has no fear of being challenged by this future of freedom, since he knows that God, too, is liberation. And by virtue of this challenge he will establish dialectical relationships with politics because he knows that what is important is not the form taken by politics or the Church, but the march towards liberty, which concerns them both. The alternative proposed by these Christians cannot be dubbed a 'clericalism of the Left' because they do not give absolute value to any political form, since they subordinate everything to the total liberation that is the presupposition of their political actions and of their relationship to the Church.

The Church of the *aggiornamento,* for its part, undoubtedly scarred from its deadly experience in the Franco era, and swayed by a theology currently in vogue that seeks to place the Church 'above the hurly-burly', is trying to find its identity by abstracting itself from historical events. I have tried to show why this is an impossible venture. It condemns the Church to being always in the rear of what is happening and to earning the sobriquet of opportunism. This danger is already a sad reality. In these early days of our democracy, the progressive lay forces in the Spanish State are constantly denouncing and resisting the violence being done by the current reforms to a whole series of human rights: arbitrary discrimination in legalizing workers' political parties and Socialist unions, contempt for the rights of ethnic minorities; not to mention the apathy shown by the Church to the proposed total amnesty.

One can argue that things will get better, that it is a question of the pace at which best to proceed, and so on. But the reality is that things are being achieved little by little, due to the mobilization of the people, to the struggles of parties and unions, and also, unfortunately, at the cost of many lives. Lamentations after the event, so characteristic of this Church, are not what is needed. It is no use waiting for quieter times, dreaming of a clarification of roles that will put everything neatly in place: politics with politics and the Church with its God. Roles are never assigned in this way, because history shows that freedom always falls victim to troubled times. The liberty of the poor is a challenge thrown down to politics, but also to the Christian faith. And in Spain we have reached a critical moment: if liberty is to be credible as an ideal it must not be divorced from freedom now, but built on it.

Translated by Paul Burns

Osmund Schreuder

The Silent Majority

INTRODUCTION

IN RECENT years, theologians have been concerned about whether
Christian preaching is really effective. In their opinion, preaching is
one of the most important tasks that the Churches can carry out, but
they are aware that the Churches are not able to exert much influence
outside the church buildings themselves. They are also aware of the
increasing competition from other ideologies, for example, and the
immensely powerful mass media. They have therefore regretfully to
admit that the outlook for Christian preaching is certainly not rosy.
There has consequently been a good deal of discussion lately about the
defects in the form and content of preaching. The phrase 'crisis in the
Churches' preaching' has even been used.

In this crisis, an appeal has been made to those specializing in
sociological research, but the latter have unfortunately done very little
work on the theme of preaching. There have been very few studies in
this sphere and most of them have consisted of a fairly superficial list of
complaints and wishes or else of a more profound analysis of the content of sermons. In very few studies indeed has the relationship between the sermon and the listeners been examined and in almost every
case these studies have considerable methodological shortcomings.
For these reasons, then, what sociologists have to tell us about preaching today is only of relative importance. Some of these sociological
studies are simply impressionistic. Others are based on a general application of the theory of mass communication. Finally, there are several
which are the result of dubious or restricted research.

11

AN EXPLORATION INTO THE FIELD

The statements made about preaching in this article also have a restricted empirical basis. They are in fact based on a very broad survey conducted among 2,500 Catholics and Protestants and an observation of 50 sermons (including 50 interviews per sermon). The survey was carried out, from the methodological and technical point of view, in a professional way.[1] Unfortunately, the survey is already ten years old and was carried out in the Federal Republic of Germany. It is not representative of the German Catholic and Protestant population or of the active church membership. We are therefore bound to conclude that the statements based on the Catholic interviews in this survey[2] are really no more than a series of serious hypotheses, because their universal validity has not yet been proved. They are, however, serious and it is worthwhile discussing them here, because they have been taken from an extensive and careful survey.

In my exploration, I have taken a kind of market model as my point of departure. Preachers try, in a sense, to dispose of their 'goods' by arranging the form and content of their sermons. Different listeners have different needs, wishes and experiences and these determine the nature of the sermon. The results of this process of supply and demand can be measured by the listeners' response to the sermon, their attentiveness, appreciation and recollection of its contents.

In the following sections, I shall consider the separate complexes and their interrelationship. I begin with the question of demand and then analyze the question of supply.

EXPERIENCES AND EXPECTATIONS

The first requisite for the success of the sermon with the congregation is the experience that the latter has of the sermon as an institution. It would seem, however, that there is no real barrier to the sermon as such. This is contrary to what has often been assumed. Church-goers are for the most part positive in their attitude towards what they hear from the pulpit on Sundays. Only a minority is clearly dissatisfied. This finding does not point to a universal feeling of uneasiness about the sermon.

This impression is confirmed by the evidence that there is no general desire to replace the sermon by other forms of religious communication such as religious broadcasts on the radio and television, religious reading, courses or group discussions. The majority is in favour of the sermon. It is, of course, true that there is, generally speaking, no deep reason for favouring the sermon. What is often mentioned is the 'religious atmosphere in the church'. On the other hand, there are no clear primary reasons given by those who do not favour the sermon. Their reasons are also mainly related to secondary aspects such as the technical possibilities of television, rather than to the content of the sermon itself. To summarize, then, the institution of the sermon would seem to be very strong compared with other means of religious communication. Only a minority seems to be in favour of other means such as religious courses and group discussions, in which they can themselves take part.

The sermon as an institution is relatively little criticized by churchgoers, at least explicitly, because of the high degree of homogeneity that exists among them with regard to expectations and criteria of appreciation. This homogeneity is surprising in view of the fact that church-goers form a relatively mixed group from the religious and social point of view.

As far as their expectations are concerned, members of church congregations distinguish between four kinds of sermon. The first category includes sermons about God's love which aim to give the listeners strength to go on living and to comfort them in their disappointments. The second group consists of sermons on the duties and responsibilities of everyday life and especially those towards one's fellow men in one's immediate environment. The third kind of sermon is concerned with Christian doctrine or the mysteries of faith and the fourth kind deals with social and political questions from a Christian point of view. The first category of sermon is the most popular and the fourth category is the least popular with congregations, but there are no really great differences between preferences and no serious competition between them.

As far as the criteria of appreciation are concerned, a distinction is made here too between four aspects. In the first place, sermons are described as interesting or uninteresting, that is, concrete, practical, in touch with life and stimulating or the opposite. Secondly, they are regarded as pleasant or unpleasant, in other words, the preacher's tone is either friendly, modest and tolerant or the opposite. Thirdly, it is possible or not possible to believe in them. They are credible if the preacher gives an impression of conviction. In the fourth place, the sermon is appreciated if it has a clear and logical structure.

The only important criterion of appreciation that is applied to the sermon is, however, the first. If the sermons that one generally hears are interesting, they are usually found to be pleasant and credible. The opposite also applies. The most decisive criterion, as far as most members of congregations are concerned, is whether the sermon is realistic, stimulating and in touch with real life. The rest is of secondary importance and even irrelevant. Clarity also plays an important part in the listeners' judgment of the sermon, but has, as such, no influence on the degree of appreciation. It would seem, then, that most church-goers listen not with their intellect, but with their hearts and the heart has its own logic.

We may summarize this section by saying that there is a certain image of the preacher. He has to follow an explicit strategy Sunday after Sunday in an attempt to break through the barrier of anti-preaching attitudes. He has to force his way through the power of the mass media. He is so confronted with such differing and even con-tradictory expectations that no one is pleased in the congregation and he is subject to constant criticism. This image, however, would seem to be a completely false one. According to the results of our survey, it is not at all in accordance with the truth of the situation.

TYPES OF LISTENERS

Those who listen to sermons form, as we have already said, a very mixed group. They can be subdivided, for example, on the basis of their attitudes to authority. Heteronomous church-goers, it would seem from our survey, stress the authority of the Church, have a posi-tive view of the carrying out of duties, reject criticism of the Church as an institution and are not in favour of democratization, religious pluralism or the renewal of the Church. These attitudes are in striking contrast to those of more autonomous members of the Churches.

A distinction can also be made on the basis of the extent to which the church members in question are associated with their own church group or institution as such. People who are firmly associated with a group or the institution stress the need for religious practice, the impor-tance of sharing in the life of the community, the difference between Protestants and Catholics and that between Christians and non-Christians. These attitudes, too, are in clear contrast to those who are less strongly tied to the group or institution or who are more cos-mopolitan in their thinking.

These two criteria are in no sense identical, with the result that they can be combined and listeners to sermons can be subdivided into six types. At the two extremes, Type 1 is very submissive and feels strongly tied to the group or institution, whereas Type 6 is extremely autonomous and cosmopolitan in attitude.

There are some important consequences and, in some cases, no important consequences at all resulting from the religious differences outlined above. These differences seem to have little influence on the listeners' expectations and criteria of appreciation. It is true, of course, that Type 6 is more in favour of sermons that are critical of society, whereas Type 1 is not. The majority of listeners, however, those who belong to groups 2, 3, 4 and 5, have no pronounced preferences, are open to 'everything' or else let 'everything' wash over them.

These differences have more consequences, however, for the appreciation of sermons. The more heteronomous the listener is, the more satisfied he tends to be with the situation as it is and the same applies to the listener who is closely tied to his own religious group or institution. A minority of autonomous and cosmopolitan listeners are ill at ease with the existing situation and prefer religious courses and group discussions to sermons. These people also claim to suffer more than others from tensions between the claims of life and the claims of faith and to need to look more urgently for solutions to the problems to which these tensions give rise.

It is possible to situate these different religious types and the corresponding degrees of satisfaction with preaching. Religious heteronomy and a strong association with one's own group or institutional Church, together with a high level of satisfaction with preaching are found especially among older church-goers, people who live in the country or small towns, members of the lower social strata and less well educated members of the Churches. Religious autonomy, a cosmopolitan attitude and a feeling of unease are found above all among younger people, large town dwellers, members of the upper middle and the new middle classes and those with higher education (intellectuals and semi-intellectuals).

CONCRETE REACTIONS

Now that I have sketched in the general background to this problem, I can examine the reactions of the interviewees to the sermons included in the survey.

Once again, preachers are seen to be very highly regarded by their listeners, the majority of whom listen to the whole sermon attentively and have a positive appreciation of it. Only a minority of church-goers seem to be inattentive and negative in their judgment. As would be expected, there is a higher degree of attentiveness and appreciation among the more heteronomous members of the congregations.

The interviews showed that it is an entirely different matter with regard to remembering the content of the sermon. Only a minority of those interviewed about a sermon that they had heard on the day of the interview were capable of reproducing the fundamental ideas contained in the sermon. The majority of listeners were either completely unable to remember anything of it or else only able to reproduce a few fragments. Recollection of the sermon was good only when three factors were present: when the interviewees had a higher than average education, when they were very autonomous in their thinking and when they were firmly tied to the group or institution.

Another fact that emerged from the interviews was that recollection and appreciation were independent of each other. In other words, a good memory can go together with a low level of appreciation and a high level of appreciation of the sermon does not necessarily mean that it is remembered well.

THE INFLUENCE OF THE QUALITIES OF THE SERMON

We must now turn to the aspect of supply and the influence of the qualities of the sermon itself on appreciation, attentiveness and recollection.

It is possible to break the sermons included in the survey down into four groups based on their contents. First, there are those with a markedly biblical character. Second, there are those with a message transcending this world. Third, there is a group of sermons which are related to the world as the listeners experience it and fourth, there are the sermons in which faith is confronted with life.

Similarly, it is also possible to distinguish four characteristics in the form of sermons. First, there is the use of gestures, acting techniques such as mimicry and the voice (variations in tempo, modulation and so on). Second, there is clarity of the structure of the sermon. Third, there is the preacher's own view (optimistic or pessimistic) of man and the world and, finally, the preacher's tone and style (humane, personal, sympathetic and democratic or the opposite). In addition to these two groups of four categories, various other data were taken into account in the survey. One of these data was the length of the sermon.

A number of important statements have to be made in connection with the appreciation of the sermons analyzed and arranged according to the characteristics outlined above. To judge by the results of our survey, these characteristics had relatively little influence on the listeners' appreciation of the sermon. Generally speaking, it is true to say that it makes very little difference to appreciation whether the sermons are or are not biblically based, whether they are directly linked to or have no point of contact with the world as experienced by the listeners or whether they have a clear structure, are human and so on. For it to receive a high degree or a low degree of appreciation, a sermon must be either 'very good' or 'very bad'. What is not clear, however, is in what respect or respects that sermon is 'very good' or 'very bad'.

There is one exception, however, to the rule defined above and that is that the listeners proved to be relatively sensitive to the quality of the preacher's delivery. A good delivery meant a greater degree of appreciation of the sermon, a poor delivery meant that the sermon was less appreciated.

Even this question of delivery, however, was only of relative importance. All in all, the individual characteristics outlined at the beginning of this section were shown in the survey to be of very little importance to the appreciation of the sermon, which was primarily and overwhelmingly determined by the religious attitude of the members of the congregation. Once again, I have to affirm that a high level of appreciation was to a great extent dependent on the heteronomous attitude of the listeners and whether they were closely tied to their own group or Church institution. Again, it emerged clearly that a low degree of appreciation resulted from an autonomous and cosmopolitan religious attitude.

These statements apply to all six types of listeners. It was not a question of heteronomous church-goers judging sermons on the basis of their feeling of solidarity with their own Church, nor was it a question of autonomous listeners being more concerned with the qualities of the sermon itself. On the contrary, the decisive factor in all six categories of listener was not the objective reality of the sermon, but the subjective religious and Church attitude of the listeners.

This can be linked to another factor, namely that appreciation of the sermon was shown to be hardly ever the result of a conscious equation of supply and demand. There were no indications at all in our survey that a congruence between expectations and wishes on the part of the listeners on the one hand and the various qualities of the sermon itself on the other resulted in a higher level of appreciation. Nor was there any indication that the absence of such a congruence resulted in a lower degree of appreciation.

To summarize, then, I may say with certainty, on the basis of our survey, that if the preacher has a reasonable delivery, his listeners will give him a great deal of liberty in the form and content of his sermons. This is because appreciation on the part of the listeners is not determined by the qualities of the sermon, but by their feelings of solidarity with the preacher. The majority of those who hear sermons are already on the side of the preacher, who is certainly not placed in a market situation and does not have to convince his critical listeners by the high quality of what he is supplying. The results of our survey may be a comfort to some preachers, but they may, of course, disappoint others.

The question of attentiveness and recollection is slightly different. The listeners are more attentive and remember more if the sermon is more closely linked to the world as they know it, if the message proclaimed is not transcendent and if the sermon has a clear structure. The other characteristics of the sermon as listed at the beginning of this section have no influence on the attentiveness and recollection of the listeners. Even the preacher's delivery has no influence. We will conclude this section with one comment—church-goers attend to biblical based sermons, but find them difficult to remember.

THE IMAGE OF THE PREACHER

It is generally accepted in the sphere of mass communications that the 'image' of the broadcaster has an influence on the reactions of those who receive his message. This also applies to preaching. Whether the congregation has already heard the preacher or not or whether or not he is known to the people seems to be unimportant here. These factors neither increase nor decrease the attention of the listeners or their appreciation of the sermon. What is of decisive importance is what the people in the church think of the preacher as a pastor, in other words, what they think of the way in which he carries out his task as a whole. If they have a positive evaluation of this, they will listen attentively to his sermons and appreciate them. It is, of course, the more heteronomous church-goers, who feel a closer link with their own group or institution, who evaluate their pastor-preacher positively. The process of preaching is thus clearly seen to be something that is in no sense isolated.

Whether the people remember the contents of their preacher's sermons has nothing to do with the image that they have of him.

CONCLUSION

Although it was not representative, our exploration into the field of preaching was extensive and exact. It also shows that there is a 'crisis in the Churches' preaching'. Our definition of 'crisis' in this context is different, however, from that commonly provided by theologians, self-critical pastors and lay intellectuals. According to my study, 'crisis' does not mean that the mass of church-goers have very uneasy feelings about the sermons that they hear because their preachers are failing in their task of preaching. On the contrary, our interviews have shown clearly that the mass of church-goers form a 'silent majority' with a predominantly positive evaluation of the situation as it is.

On the basis of the same exploration, however, I am bound to say that it is precisely this positive evaluation of preaching that is in itself a problem. On closer inspection, it is clear that this speaking on the part of the 'silent majority' contains a great deal of silence. I can express this less cryptically by saying that the 'crisis in the Churches' preaching' can be traced to the almost entirely unconscious and non-explicit attitudes on the part of the mass of church-goers towards sermons and preaching, with the result that there is a fairly undifferentiated reaction to the supply offered by preachers and very little of the 'goods' is taken away, despite all the care that pastors devote to their sermons. The problem, then, is to be found less in the pulpit itself and more in the body of the Church.

The aspects of this crisis that we have characterized in this article by the deliberately ambiguous title 'The Silent Majority' can, of course, be formulated differently. The 'crisis in the Churches' preaching' has come about because the Churches' preachers are confronted with a mass of people whose feelings of solidarity are characterized by unarticulated totality. This prevents the Churches from functioning in a differentiated way for their members. They may programme their supply of pastoral care as much as they like and present it in many different ways, but all these various programmes are assimilated by the mass of people with a 'blind' solidarity, which is insensitive to differentiation and therefore acts as a brake on the effectiveness of these programmes. In my exploration, I have illustrated this principle by using the model of preaching.

Translated by David Smith

Notes

1. The author of this article was generally in charge of this survey. The day-to-day guidance was in the hands of J. Sterk. The following contributed to the preparation of the field study and helped to carry it out: L. Bertsch, K. W. Bühler, K. Bergsmüller, K. W. Dahm, R. Köster and R. Zerfass.

2. For a detailed report on the Catholic part of the survey, which was based on 1231 interviews and 25 sermons, see J. Sterk, *Preek en toehoorders* (Nijmegen, Instituut voor Toegepaste Sociologie, 1975). This article is largely based on this report. The conclusions for the Protestant part are to a great extent the same; the two parts only differ in secondary details.

PART II

Communication Across Frontiers

Brian Smith

The Impact of Foreign Church Aid:
The Case of Chile

SINCE THE late nineteen-fifties there has been a significant increase in the transfer of personnel and finances from churches in the North Atlantic region to those in third-world countries. The United States, for example, doubled the number of its missionaries in Latin America between 1958 and 1968. Various overseas aid organizations supported by Catholics in North America and Western Europe have increased the flow of financial and material resources to Churches in Asia, Africa and Latin America in the last fifteen years. Such increased personnel and monetary aid has enabled these Churches to inaugurate pro- grammes of religious and social development that they could not have undertaken on their own.

Such assistance has, however, come under strong criticism. Some blame foreigners for imposing their cultural values on the churches where they serve, for artificially maintaining outdated structures, and for preventing church leaders in developing countries from searching for their indigenous and creative solutions to their problems.[1] Others have argued that foreign money maintains these churches in a pro- longed state of dependency and also allows foreign donors to control their style of religious and ideological development.[2] Governments have increasingly become suspicious of their intentions of foreign priests in many areas and in recent years have expelled significant numbers for allegedly interfering in the internal political affairs of their countries.

So far there has been little study done over time on the amounts of foreign personnel and finances given to third-world Churches in comparison with the indigenous sources of support they have been able to generate. Such data is important for determining if progress is being made in developing more autonomy, a factor which will give these Churches greater freedom to choose their own priorities and also make them less vulnerable to political criticism. Insufficient attention has also been paid to the judgments of religious leaders in these countries on the impact of foreign assistance. Many of the criticisms thus far have been made by those who have no pastoral responsibility in Churches receiving this aid.

The Chilean Church offers a good case in which to examine the substance of these criticisms. Over the past fifteen years it has been one of the most active Churches in developing countries in efforts to implement the pastoral and social emphases of Vatican II (and Medellín)—sharing responsibilities with the laity, formation of small basic communities, involvement with the problems of the working classes, the promotion of human rights. It has been a major actor in the rapid social and political changes in that country under three different political regimes: Christian Democratic (1964–1970), Marxist Socialist (1970–1973), and authoritarian military (1973—). It has received substantial amounts of outside help, but since the mid-1960's has defined as one of its major goals the development of autonomous support.

FOREIGN MISSIONARIES

In 1975 as part of a larger research project on the Chilean Church I gathered empirical data on changing patterns of external vs. internal resources over the past decade. In structured interviews with all thirty active bishops, with a stratified sample of seventy-two priests throughout the country, with thirty-three nuns engaged in parish work in seven of the twenty-four dioceses, and with fifty-one men and women active in small basic communities among different social classes (mainly in Santiago), I included questions to discover their judgments on the impact of foreign clergy and money on the Chilean Church in recent years.

Table 1 indicates that there was a large influx of foreign priests into Chile during the nineteen-fifties. In the period of rapid religious, social and political change in the nineteen-sixties and early seventies these foreigners constituted approximately one-half of the clergy, and native vocations to the priesthood have not increased significantly over the past fifteen years. After 1973 there was a substantial decline in the number of priests in the country (a net loss of 380, or 15% of the total), due mostly to the decrease of foreigners.

Table 1:   *Nationality of Clergy in Chile, 1945–1975*

Year	Chilean Priests	Foreign Priests	Totals
1945	1,098 (60.7%)	711 (39.8%)	1,809
1960	1,159 (49.5%)	1,183 (50.5%)	2,342
1965	1,140 (48.6%)	1,207 (51.4%)	2,347
1973	1,289 (51.7%)	1,202 (48.3%)	2,491
1975	1,223 (57.9%)	888 (42.1%)	2,111

When asked how they would evaluate the performance of foreign priests, close to one half (46.9%) of all the respondents in my interviews felt that they had provided very effective support for the Chilean Church. Sixty percent of the priests and 54.8% of the nuns, however, said that many did not adjust well to Chile or wasted much of their energies by becoming involved in too many activities.[3] Over two-fifths of the hierarchy (44.8%) expressed similar judgments, and more than one bishop voiced the opinion that some foreigners came to Chile in order to work out frustrations with more conservative Churches in their home countries or to engage in social and political activism.

The bishops have assigned most foreign priests to the poorest parishes, and amidst intense social and political change, they identified with the whole gamut of the problems affecting their congregations. Approximately 150 foreigners, however, were expelled after the military coup for allegedly having engaged in partisan political activities during the Allende régime, and many more left Chile on their own accord or at the urging of the hierarchy for their own safety. Many of these foreigners were active in 'Christians for Socialism', a movement made up mostly of clerics (the majority of whom were from working-class parishes), who publicly endorsed efforts by the *Unidad Popular* government to effect a transition to socialism. They attempted as part of their ministry to raise the political consciousness of their parishioners and mobilize support for many government projects, while disclaiming any specific party affiliation.

While two-thirds of the bishops in the twenty dioceses that lost foreign priests since 1973 felt that it is better that they have gone, since they were controversial, the majority of the priests, nuns, and lay leaders in these areas indicated either that the loss has been crucial for the Church or that in many instances the expulsions were unfair since these men were doing good pastoral work.

Despite the substantial number of foreigners in Chile since 1960, I found no indication that this has prevented a creative use of local personnel, or served to maintain outdated structures. Although vocations to the priesthood have not increased, currently there are about two hundred married deacons many of whom are responsible for territories where there are not enough priests. Eighty of the 760 parishes in the country are now under the exclusive pastoral care of women religious who administer all the sacraments except the Eucharist and the Sacrament of Reconciliation. There are also 50,000 lay catechists (mostly women) being trained in small study circles in their respective neighborhoods in order to prepare their own children for the sacraments. About 20,000 committed lay men and women are carrying on the daily religious and social activities of various types of base communities throughout the country. All of these developments have occurred as a result of decisions by the hierarchy after Vatican II to decentralize church structures and share more pastoral responsibilities with laity and religious. Foreigners and nationals alike have worked in close cooperation with the bishops to make this real.

FINANCIAL AID

The Chilean Church has not, however, made significant progress during this period in generating an autonomous base of financial support. In 1964 the bishops inaugurated a form of tithing to replace parish collections which traditionally have been small since only 12% of Catholics fulfil their Sunday obligation. The hierarchy asked all families to contribute 1% of their annual income to the Church. This programme, known as Contribution to the Church (CALI), has produced a twelve-year total of only $3.2 million between 1964 and 1975.

Although there have been other internal sources of financing (rents, interests on investments, donations to popular religious shrines, salaries for priests teaching religion in public schools), the bishops indicated in my interviews with them that these are small and together with CALI provide for little more than maintenance costs for existing buildings and living expenses for clergy. Everything in the area of religious and social development—leadership formation, new catechetical programmes, research institutes, technical training for peasants and workers, construction, health and nutrition projects, and more recently legal and economic assistance to political prisoners and their families—has required very large amounts of outside church support.

Between 1964 and 1975, for example, Catholic Relief Services in the United States has donated food, clothing and medicine to Chilean Church projects to the value of $47.4 million. Misereor in West Germany has given $5.7 million for projects to alleviate hunger and disease. Adveniat (also in West Germany) has sent $9.4 million, and the US Catholic Conference over $900,000, for pastoral leadership training, catechetical programmes, and religious and social research. Between 1969 and 1975 other Catholic overseas aid agencies in Canada, Belgium, Great Britain, France, the Netherlands, Switzerland, Austria, Ireland and Luxembourg contributed a total of $2.9 million to social and economic development projects of the Chilean Church. In addition, during the first two years after the military coup of September, 1973, the World Council of Churches gave or channelled approximately $1.5 million to support various human rights projects sponsored by the Chilean Catholic Church in co-operation with several other religious denominations in the country.

When asked their opinion of the impact of such foreign assistance, almost none of the respondents in my interviews complained of attempts to control the Chilean Church by donor organizations. Two bishops indicated that grants are given for very specific projects chosen according to the interests of foreign agencies, and these bishops expressed a belief that this has limited the flexibility of Chileans in using the money for their self-defined priorities.

Two-fifths of the priests, nuns, and lay leaders, however, felt that this aid has artificially maintained the Church and prevented it from confronting its financial problems realistically.[4] One-half of the hierarchy believed such aid was completely justified since the Chilean Church at present is unable to support itself, but a substantial minority (42.9%) said that foreign assistance must only be a temporary measure until local resources are adequately developed.

The problem is that, given the availability of such large amounts of foreign money, there is insufficient motivation to generate more local financial resources. Several bishops complained that many priests have not promoted CALI aggressively in their parishes. While it is a fact that the vast majority of foreigners do work in poor areas of the country, it is also true that many receive substantial amounts of support from their home dioceses or religious congregations abroad. This aid diminishes their motivation to move in the direction of making their parishes more financially autonomous.

The Chilean laity have also been unresponsive to the hierarchy's appeal for support. While two-thirds of the population are in the working class and very poor, there are many other families who could donate to CALI and who do not. Between 1964 and 1973 the average number of heads of households contributing to this program was 53,000. While the number has almost doubled since the coup in late 1973, this still represents less than 6% of all Catholic families in the country.

In addition, both ends of the political spectrum in Chile have severely criticized the Church for how it has used some of its foreign financial support. During the mid-nineteen-sixties Communists and Socialists maintained that large amounts of aid were being used to disseminate anti-Marxist ideology and train peasants and workers with strong sympathies for Christian Democracy. Since the coup in 1973 rightists and supporters of the military junta have bitterly attacked the Church in the state-controlled media for assisting Marxists and other opponents of the present régime in many of its projects for the poor and the persecuted. Both criticisms contain elements of truth, and the intention of some foreign donors to the Chilean Church has been to help accomplish each of these different objectives under different circumstances.

While overt foreign control as such is not the problem, the fact that part of this international aid has been made available for specific projects that seem to favour certain groups or ideological positions in Chile more than others does make the local Church vulnerable to criticism (especially in times of political polarization). It also makes it appear to some as the agent of a foreign power. While a strong and strictly pastoral argument can be made in favour of the various humanitarian projects the Chilean Church is now promoting, the fact that these legal and economic programs are almost entirely financed by foreign support has heightened already severe tensions between Church and state. The present military régime has made efforts to curtail and control the influx of international Church money into the country and at times has harassed those who are dispersing it in Chile.

CONCLUSION

On the basis of the experience of the Chilean Church since 1960 and the judgments of various groups of its leadership, it appears that whereas some of the arguments made against foreign Church aid are not necessarily valid, others are cogent. When a national hierarchy exercises leadership and imagination in pastoral innovation, large numbers of foreign personnel need not be an obstacle to the creation of new structures and types of leadership with roots in the national culture. When foreign priests, however, constitute a large proportion of the clergy and also become closely involved in the social and political struggles of the poor whom they serve, authoritarian régimes can substantially reduce an important sector of the leadership of the Church by simply revoking the visas of foreign priests whom they consider troublesome.

While foreign money enables a Church in a developing area to initiate religious and social projects it would not be capable of starting on its own, the continued heavy dependence of these programmes on outside support can lead to some serious problems. At times such aid does reflect the inherent ideological preferences of the donors and cannot help but have significant political consequences in the host country, depending upon the context and uses to which it is put. Furthermore, such aid reduces the motivation of those who are capable of contributing to the support of their local Church to do so and thus to identify more closely with its struggles and goals.

It is clear that Churches such as that of Chile at present require outside financial and personnel support to carry on essential religious and social projects needed by their people, especially the poor and oppressed. Until such Churches can stimulate more indigenous and autonomous bases of support, however, their independence and freedom will remain curtailed.

Notes

1. The most outspoken proponent of these criticisms has been Ivan Illich. (Cf., I. Illich, 'The Seamy Side of Charity', *America* 116 (1967), 88–91.)

2. D. E. Mutchler, *The Church as a Political Factor in Latin America: With Particular Reference to Colombia and Chile* (New York, 1971).

3. Chilean priests and nuns were significantly more critical of foreign clergy than foreigners themselves in my survey. Seventy percent of the Chilean priests as opposed to 51.7% of the foreigners expressed these negative judgments of foreign-born clergy. Among the sisters, 61.6% of the Chileans compared to 50% of the foreigners voiced such opinions.

4. On this question, the foreign priests and nuns were more critical in their judgments than their Chilean counterparts. Among the priests, 45.2% of the foreigners as contrasted to 36.6% of the nationals felt external aid was an artificial solution. In the sample of nuns, 47.1% of those from abroad in comparison to only 30% of the native sisters believed foreign money had a negative impact on the Chilean Church. Hence, while Chilean priests and nuns are rather critical of the performance of foreign personnel (cf. note 3), they are more content to accept foreign money.

Kenneth Westhues

Nationalism and Canadian Catholicism

THE VICTORY of a separatist party in the Quebec election of 1976 both demonstrated and aggravated the fragility of Canadian national unity. The process of national integration has not progressed far enough in Canada to ensure that it will survive intact. From within, the country is weakened by Quebec's claim to self-determination, a claim echoed to a lesser but still significant extent by the western and maritime provinces. From without, national autonomy is undermined by dependence on the United States for capital, commodities, culture and defence. Both internal cleavages and external dependency have delayed nation-building in Canada, the future of which remains in doubt even as it enters the second decade of its second century. The purposes of this article is to describe the rôle of the Catholic Church in the process of political integration in the Canadian milieu.

HISTORICAL BACKGROUND

Of the 22 million Canadians in 1971, the Catholic Church claimed 46%, a proportion slightly larger than a hundred years previous.[1] Currently, about 58% of the Catholic population is of French ancestry, 20% of British including Irish, 7% of Italian, and the remainder spread across Amerindian, Dutch, German, Polish, Portuguese, Ukrainian and other ethnic backgrounds. The Church counts members in each of the ten provinces, its share of the population ranging from 87% in Quebec to 19% in British Columbia. The provincial governments, which control and finance education, use tax revenues to provide varying degrees of support to Catholic schools and universities. The sixty-two dioceses of the Canadian Church have, at least until recent years, found more than sufficient candidates for the priesthood, and a diverse array of religious orders has generally flourished. For all of these reasons, the Catholic Church is the pre-eminent religious institution of Canadian society, an institution whose social policy and internal politics necessarily have implications in secular affairs.

In principle, Rome has sought throughout the world to reinforce those political boundaries which facilitate its mission and to weaken those boundaries which obstruct it. In the Canadian context, this principle has called for a double nationalism. First, the Church has guarded the boundary separating Canada from the United States more carefully than almost any other Canadian organization. The Quebec Act of 1774 and the British North America Act of 1867 granted the Church far greater security than did the American constitution. The former guaranteed to the Church public support of its schools and at least partial recognition of its parish structure, while the latter reduced it to a voluntary association obliged to compete with other private groups for the participation of members. It was thus in the Church's interest to minimize the lines of communication between its Canadian and American branches. Indeed, this happened. Only two present-day Canadian bishops were born in the United States, seminarians have seldom been sent south for their education, and the Canadian Church has chosen to maintain its own periodicals rather than rely on those of its larger American counterpart. To the extent that the border has been crossed, it has meant Canadian penetration of the American Church as frequently as *vice versa*.

If the Church's first nationalism strengthens the Canadian fact, its second nationalism enfeebles it. The latter is a defence of the border which separates Quebec from the other, predominantly Anglophone provinces and which seeks to preserve the French reality in a largely self-contained region within Canada. The privileges the Church enjoys in the country at large all derive historically from the concessions made by the British Crown to the bishop and priests of Quebec at the time of the Conquest. Faced with ruling a colony of conquered French Catholics, the British Empire granted the Church unprecedented prerogatives, even the right to collect tithes, in return for its pledge to secure the loyalty of the colony to the British Crown.[2] Because it was the French language that permitted the Church such extraordinary influence, and because the linguistic barrier was almost all that prevented Francophone Canadians from assimilation into Protestant North America, the Church rightly regarded the language as guardian of the faith. Politically, this required above all the maintenance of autonomy for the Quebec province and a certain isolation of the Quebec Church from its counterpart in English Canada. While the Church was ready to support an incipient Canadian nation against its secular southern neighbour, it was anxious to foster the long-established Quebeçoise nation all the more.

Whereas the Church succeeded in becoming part of the fabric of Quebec society, this was not the case anywhere else in Canada. An attempt to create a miniature replica of Quebec on the banks of the Red River in present-day Manitoba failed, and the province came to be dominated by Protestants. For all the settlements of French, Scottish, Irish, German and Ukrainian Catholics outside Quebec, there was nothing to do but send priests of appropriate ethnicity to minister to them. When parishes and dioceses were eventually established in these mainly Anglophone areas, they assumed the character of the relevant Catholic minority. For the most part, provincial governments interpreted the rights of the Church in education as belonging not to the hierarchy but to the Catholic people, and placed Catholic schools under lay control. The result was that in Quebec the Church was at home, while the rest of Canada was a diaspora.

THE BI-PARTITE CHURCH

Given the legacy of its past, there has been no reason for the Church in Canada to become a nationally cohesive organization, nor to overcome the communications problem of the French-English barrier. The federal government has preferred, if anything, the segmentation of the Church across the provinces and regions, lest it be compelled to recognize on a national scale what has long been the case in Quebec. Rome itself, until the past two decades, showed little interest in national bishops' assemblies, and was generally content to treat each diocese as a discrete and autonomous ecclesiastical entity; the traditional theology of the episcopate was congruent with such a policy. Within Canada, moreover, the Quebec hierarchy feared any contact with Anglophone Canada which might dilute the strength of Quebec Catholicism; for their part, the bishops of the diaspora feared domination by their understandably disdainful brothers in Quebec. To the extent, therefore, that one can speak of a Canadian Church, it is really no more than an aggregate of bishops facing disparate problems in diverse legal and cultural milieus. The following paragraphs review some of the barriers dividing the linguistic branches of Canadian Catholicism.

The Canadian dioceses fall into three broad categories. The first embraces the eighteen within the borders of Quebec. Fifteen of these embrace populations at least 90% Catholic, while the remaining three are at least 75% Catholic. The median size of the Quebec dioceses is about 150,000 people. A second category includes the sixteen dioceses which are outside Quebec but predominantly Francophone. These tend to be in rural areas, and appear to have been formed in such a way as to circumscribe French minorities in Anglophone environments; their median size is exceedingly small, about 38,000 Catholic people. The third category is composed of the remaining twenty-seven dioceses, predominantly Anglophone and larger, both in area and in population (median size about 75,000 Catholics). In almost none of these do Catholics constitute a majority of the population; the Anglophone dioceses are also more urban than the French dioceses outside Quebec.

The importance of an overwhelmingly Catholic population within a diocese, independent of cultural and legal factors, deserves emphasis. The experience of being a Catholic differs markedly between that setting in which 'everyone is Catholic' and that in which most are not. In the former, the Church is perceived as a fact of life, a symbolic centre for the entire community, even for those who seldom attend church.[3] In the minority setting, the Church is perceived necessarily as a voluntary creation of its members, a source of community division rather than solidarity, and an affiliation about which members cannot help but be defensive. For the hierarchy, the homogeneous setting provides an opportunity to influence diverse aspects of social life; the Quebec bishops' involvement in the establishment of parish-based credit unions and cooperatives during the nineteen-thirties is a case in point.[4] In the minority setting, such hierarchical efforts are never so successful, because they depend on the self-segregation of Catholics from friends and neighbours in the same political and economic situation. The simple difference in the proportion of Catholics in the diocesan population is a major divisive influence between French and English Catholicism in Canada, and one which exacerbates the difference in language.[5]

Added to the differences in language and majority-minority status between the Quebec dioceses and those in the other provinces is the difference in formal legal status. Quebec civil law has recognized the canonical parish since the French colonial era; the parish thus becomes an administrative unit in public administration in the province and retains a public institutional status to this day.[6] The public educational system of Quebec, moreover, remained under firm church control until the nineteen-sixties, and it is by no means secular even now.[7] In the other provinces, even those which provide government money to Catholic schools, the Church is not a public institution but fundamentally a voluntary association. In Quebec, as in the nations of South America, the Church can be praised or condemned, but it has touched the culture too intimately to be ignored. In the rest of Canada, by contrast, the Church can be more easily disregarded as an optional activity external to the cultural core.

Such divisions as these between the two arms of Canadian Catholicism might still have been mediated if the personnel policy of the Church had fostered horizontal communication across the country instead of relying on the vertical dimension linking each diocese to Rome. Such, however, has not been the case. Of the twenty-five bishops currently appointed to Quebec dioceses, twenty-one were born in that province, none were born elsewhere in Canada, and the remaining four are foreign-born. Of the forty bishops elsewhere in the country, twenty-two were born in the province of current appointment, fifteen in other provinces, and three outside Canada. Thus, while this measure suggests a degree of horizontal communication in that part of the country outside Quebec, it indicates a notable isolation of the Quebec hierarchy from that of the rest of Canada. Also noteworthy is the fact that Francophone bishops outside Quebec tend to have roots in or near the dioceses where they serve; the Quebec Church is master of its own house, but not of that of Francophones outside the province.

Another means of forging national communication links is the organization of seminaries; a pan-Canadian consciousness in the Church might have sprung from priests and bishops having had contact with the other language group in the course of their educational formation. It appears that in the past, a minority of Anglophone clergy studied in Francophone settings, but the reverse pattern occurred only rarely. By now, moreover, the two linguistic branches of the Church each has the full complement of educational institutions, including mission seminaries. Biographical data on twenty-seven contemporary bishops reveal that only five took some part of their studies in philosophy or theology in Canadian seminaries or universities outside their own language group. The dominant pattern has been education first in the linguistic region of origin within Canada, then doctoral studies in Rome or elsewhere in Europe. This pattern of education of the leaders of the Canadian Church has reinforced vertical communication with the centre but inhibited communication across the diverse Canadian regions on the periphery.

The dichotomous regional-linguistic cleavage in the Canadian Church severely retarded the creation of a permanent national bishops' conference. In light of the creation of the Latin American Episcopal Conference in 1899 and the American (US) Catholic Welfare Conference in 1919, it is remarkable that no Canadian counterpart was established until 1943. Until then, the Canadian bishops had held only quinquennial meetings in Quebec City. It was not, however, the date of creation but the structure of the Canadian Catholic Conference which best illuminated the split within the Canadian Church. For organizational purposes, the bishops came to be divided into French and English sectors, each sector electing two vice-presidents and half the members of the Administrative Board; the presidency rotated between the two language groups and there were separate secretaries-general and Commissions for Liturgy, Education, Ecumenism and so forth. The national office in Ottawa housed in effect two linguistically defined bishops' conferences, each capable of functioning more or less on its own.

THE BI-NATIONAL STATE

In summary, the church has pursued throughout Canadian history a simple policy of double nationalism, seeking simultaneously the segregation of Canada from the United States and of Quebec from English Canada. Neither for its own structure nor for Canada as a whole has it promoted integration of the linguistic communities or horizontal communication between them. This policy, however, is challenged by the events of recent decades. Improved media of transportation and communications and the growth of economic firms have hastened the economic and cultural integration of the formerly more isolated parts of Canada. The federal government has attempted greater political integration by reducing the autonomy of the provinces, fostering bilingualism, and encouraging the interpenetration of the French and English sectors. Even Rome itself, in the post-conciliar organization of the international Church, has assigned a more central rôle to nationally organized hierarchies.

In response to these pressures for nationalization, the Canadian Church has in recent years re-organized the bishops' conference, so that it is no longer so completely divided along linguistic lines. Unitary organization has been achieved in almost all the Commissions and, formally at least, in the Conference as a whole. As would be expected, the minority of bishops with experience in both French and English Canada have assumed a disproportionate share of the offices of the national conference. Especially those in Francophone dioceses outside Quebec, along with their priests and people, have much to gain from the creation of an integrated, bi-cultural Canadian Church, just as they are likely to appreciate most a similarly integrated Canadian nation. The alternative is inevitable assimilation into their Anglophone milieus, a process which has steadily accelerated in recent decades.

As pressures for nationalization in Canada have intensified, so also has their contradiction, the separatist movement of Quebec. The latter feeds upon a belief that national integration in Canada cannot be accomplished except through Anglicization; the preservation of French reality in North America is thus believed to hinge on Quebec independence. Canadian history at this juncture is the intense conflict between these opposing forces, the one promising ethnic and linguistic pluralism through the creation of a bi-lingual nation, the other through the creation of two effectively uni-lingual nations. This is the conflict which faces equally both the Canadian Church and Canada itself.

The tragedy is not just that the Church has declared its neutrality on this issue, thus divorcing itself from the major social question of Canadian history. The greater tragedy is that the Canadian Church, as the pre-eminent non-governmental structure embracing large numbers of people in each language group, can offer so little guidance by example. It has preferred in Canada the security of entrenchment in discrete ethnic enclaves to the creation of imaginative forms of multi-ethnic organization. It has restricted its own communications too much to the vertical dimension of centre-periphery, and thus cannot offer leadership to a world in which regions on the periphery are obliged by technology to communicate and interact with one another. For this reason, the Canadian Church finds itself—with respect to French-English relations—watching from the sidelines as history is made by others.

Notes

1. Quantitative data in this article have been computed from *Le Canada Ecclésiastique* (Montréal, yearly), the federal decennial censuses of population, and various biographical dictionaries.

2. For further discussion and more detailed bibliography, see K. Westhues, 'The Adaptation of the Catholic Church in Canadian Society', in S. Crysdale & L. Wheatcroft (eds.), *Religion in Canadian Society* (Toronto, 1976).

3. It must be added, however, that as late as 1965, 88% of French-Canadian Catholics attended church regularly, as compared to 69% of English-Canadian Catholics; see J. J. Mol, 'Correlates of Church-going in Canada', in Crysdale & Wheatcroft, op. cit.

4. Cf., Jean Hulliger, *L'enseignement Social des Evêques Canadiens de 1891 à 1950* (Montréal, 1958).

5. It is interesting to note an ambience similar to that in Quebec in those Anglophone dioceses, like Antigonish, where the population is overwhelmingly Catholic. It is not by chance that Antigonish hosted the Church's major involvement in economic co-operatives in English Canada; this is described in A. F. Laidlaw, *The Man from Margaree* (Toronto, 1971).

6. Cf., J.-C. Falardeau, 'The Parish as an Institutional Type', *Canadian Journal of Economics and Political Science*, 15 (August, 1949), pp. 353-67.

7. Cf., Léon Dion, *Le Bill 60 et la Société Québeçoise* (Montreal, 1967).

André Rousseau

The Political Setting of Communications between Rome and the European Churches

AS THE TITLE indicates, this article is concerned with the nature of the political framework within which it is possible to carry out a sociological analysis of communications between Rome and the churches of Europe and the West.

THE SOCIOLOGICAL COMMUNICATION PROBLEM

I shall examine the communication problem as a special case of social relations while focussing my analysis on the way in which communications between Rome and the European churches have been institutionalized.

This methodological presupposition implies another in the choice of subject-matter. 'For the churches of Europe, the main political problem is—Europe'; [1] this would be a truism if it did not very clearly show the observer the present as well as the past ground of exchanges between the Vatican and the European churches—the ground, and not merely the framework. The European setting is a base on which and in regard to which the Vatican and the European churches communicate. This base is the matter, so to speak, of those communications.

This means that I do not accept the self-interpretation which the Catholic Church sometimes offers, according to which 'the Church is not interested in politics'. The following question is central to my article: What relation is there between the expression of religious convic-

tions about European unity and the actual way in which Roman di-
plomacy operates in regard to European institutions? That relation has
to be analyzed before any overall consideration of 'communications'
between Rome and the western churches.

The first step in a sociological analysis is to depict as fully as possible
the global context of communications between partners. Here the context is a system of economic interdependence outside the direct initia-
tive of the churches but lastingly and deeply conditioning their network
of influence. Literally, 'For the European churches, the main political
problem is Europe', to the extent that political problems are always a
major problem for a church with a universalist outlook. Given this
starting-point, the question of a sociology of communications between
Rome and the western European churches no longer implies an
analysis of the functioning or dysfunctioning of communicational structures. It is rather a question of revealing and interpreting the division of
labour between the central power in Rome and the peripheral
churches, in order to define the political goals of the Catholic Church.

This last proposition requires more precise definition in order to
remove all ambiguity. There is no need to follow so many other authors
in describing the permanence and reinforcement of a dual Roman tradition, and of the bureaucratic centralism and the primacy allotted to
diplomatic action.[2] I do not intend to pass judgment on the *fact* of the
Church's engagement in politics, and still less the actual politics pursued. It is sufficient, it seems to me, to reveal evidence too often
concealed or evaded with euphemisms. In this way it is easier to understand the social relations which unite Rome and the churches of western Europe.

I shall centre my analysis on three documents. The first originates
from a student of 'European' ideology and concerns Christian action
for a United Europe. The second treats of the same subjects and emanates from the Belgian Bishops' Conference. The third is the report of a
meeting attended by a representative of the Secretariat of State of the
Holy See and representatives of the European Bishops' Conferences.[3]
The choice of these three documents is not merely pragmatic. It enables us to see the essential components of the field of interest. The
political concern here is the discourse of the 'ideological laity' of
Europe and that of the Secretariat of State. The three documents treat
of the problem of the influence of Christian ideology on European
unity. Finally, each of the documents includes 'pertinent aspects'
which contrast with the other two: lay discourse/communication between clergy; political discourse/pastoral discourse; use of the Christian message as ethics/reference to sacred sources in order to justify an
institutional order and a strategy.

THE DESIRE TO STANDARDIZE SOCIETY

'The Catholic bishops cannot abandon their duty to take an interest in the work of the European Community . . . in the light of the responsibilities which fall upon all Christians, in order to restore the moral order, justice and peace in Europe and in the world. That is possible only by qualitative change in European Christianity: that is, by the creation of a Christianity which can impregnate the social and political structures of Europe'.[4] This quotation can be replaced by many others which just as clearly show the Church's ambition to define or to contribute to a definition of the authentic European ideology. Two types of argument are invoked to justify this ambition. On the one hand, the historico-cultural tradition of the Europe which was largely constructed in the movement of Christianity itself; on the other hand, the ethical competence of the Church. In the second case, the argument consists in deducing the right of the Church to speak on the ethical nature of European problems. On the lips of a representative of the Secretariat of State, these two arguments become one when the Church is identified with the 'soul of Europe': Europe is then a body which organizes its unity round about economical and social structures which can be 'stimulants or obstacles to unification according to the spirit which is in them, according to the presence or absence of that true spirit, of that cement which ought to join the several fragments. If, latterly, the construction of Europe has slackened, it is precisely because this cement of unity, this bond of the European soul and spirit is missing. It is here that the Church is able to contribute and has the duty to offer its services generously'.[5]

As if in response to this way of posing the problem, the Belgian bishops write in regard to their 'declaration' of Europe: 'The Gospel of Christ can be a source of inspiration for all Europeans . . . It is clear that the Gospel does not offer any detailed programme in answer to twentieth-century problems and those of the next century. But anyone who reflects on matters in the light of the Good News will be all the more acutely aware of the dangers to be avoided and the goals to pursue in order to ensure that the Europe of tomorrow has a vital spirit'.[6]

There is no need to extend the list of quotations. Here we have obvious examples of a position which moulds most theologies, and whose axis, as it were, is the indispensable nature of religious truth as the foundation of the social edifice in each of its parts.[7] But, as we know, a theology may be the speculative or theoretical countenance of a politics, its 'spiritual point of honour', and an assertion of its interests. We have to analyze this kind of discourse in two complementary respects.

My working hypothesis is as follows. Catholic ideology in regard to Europe serves a division of labour on two levels: on the one hand it keeps the laity under the control of a normative thought system (of which I have cited examples) and within the field of influence of the Christian Democratic parties. On the other hand, it keeps the local episcopates ideologically dependent on Rome and thus tends to deprive the local churches of control over the European policy of the Vatican. The second aspect of the hypothesis is more pertinent to this article. In fact the two aspects of the process reinforce one another. The division of labour between Rome and the national episcopates supposes that the relation of those episcopates to their faithful also avoids the question of the influences and political strategies of the churches.

ORTHODOXY AS A REPRESENTATION OF ORTHOPRAXIS

I shall refer to orthodoxy here as a general ideological process: for intellectuals or clergy, ideology is a form of intransigent thought which does not enter into negotiation, or succeeds in obfuscating or avoiding it. This process is characteristic of ideologies because the actors in the field of influence of a movement of opinion, a political party or a church, are also most often present in other fields and open to other influences. These exchanges get back to the point of origin only through a large number of filters and, ideally, orthodoxy, the intransigent thought of the clergy, controls these exchanges, or behaves as if they did not take place.

When I say that orthodoxy operates as the representation of orthopraxis, I mean that, in this model, a question of action appears to have been formulated successfully when it is formulated within conceptual frameworks which are as faithful as possible to the beliefs of the basis of the group. In this way, which is very close to what Max Weber called 'the ethics of conviction', action is conceived only with difficulty and by means of a great number of scenarios, or as a play of alliances and oppositions. It is more often conceived as an imperative; it brings the group together, and allows it to 'meet' round its foundational message; but it hardly modifies the conditions of production of the discourse in question.

We can find many traces of this process in the declaration of the Belgian bishops. Of course the document contains a series of practical propositions with two main characteristics. On the one hand, they are formulated as imperatives: '. . . education and training *must* . . . We *must* free ourselves . . . We *must* show ourselves open . . . No one *can* tolerate . . .'[8] On the other hand, and as is already evident from the foregoing quotations, the suggestions made are offered to all, provided that everyone recognizes himself in the initial ethical imperatives. In short, this document takes for granted in its presuppositions that the hearer is of the faith, and it takes it for granted throughout.

Its function is revealed in this self-confirmation. We read the following for example: 'St. Paul writes that we are called to become free men (Gal. 5:13). Anyone who wants to liberate Europe must begin by liberating himself from everything by which he is enchained' (p. 6). And, further on: 'If we seriously believe that all human creatures are equal in the eyes of God, it is time indeed that men and women were really treated on an equal footing' (p. 10).

The mechanism of ideological production here may be analyzed as follows. Actual objectives in the political field are removed from their context. Borne by particular groups, associated with means which are, by definition, objects for discussion, in the discourse of ecclesiastical authority they lose those two characteristics and become universal moral values supplemented in a wholly arbitrary fashion with a biblical commentary. Everything proceeds as if, when faced with questions arising from the transformation of the socio-political field, religious authority were offering answers primarily intended to reinforce its own legitimacy and to reproduce the needs of its own discourse'.[9]

The effectiveness of this device is clear from the document by a 'European' ideologue.[10] There we see clearly that the laity, who are themselves ideologues in the political field,[11] can draw from religious discourse the moral resources to legitimate their political strategies. But this legitimation process involves some displacement and even obfuscation. In fact, political strategies are not designated as such: Europe, and of course Europe as it is seen by the Christian Democratic parties, becomes an ethico-religious demand: 'Faced with the problem of union, Europe is playing its destined rôle, which is that of a large part of Christendom' (p. 5). 'Before these problems (of justice), Europe has a unique rôle to play. If Christians stay away from this stage, they traduce the future' (p. 18).[12]

Here we can see the effect of ideology as described above. Political action is wholly imbued with axiology. It is of concern to the present thesis that the Church brings this 'solemn complement' to a European ideology. Two aspects need special emphasis. On the one hand, by posing political objectives in an absolute sense, that is by absolutizing what is relative, religious ideology behaves as if there were no conflict in the definition of those objectives, which are seen entirely as convictions. Once it has been put forward as a 'superior' ideal, can the European idea really, as the document supposes, serve to reconcile social layers within the Church? This ambition would be based on an alliance of Catholic intellectuals and ecclesiastical authority. Surely that is a means of leading the faithful, by the means of a gentle form of 'opinion control,' along a political path which increasingly abandoned or found highly problematical in the various countries of Europe. But, on the other hand, the schema I have analyzed in fact hides from view any real ecclesiastical influence in the social and political institutions of Europe.

FROM THE SOCIAL DIVISION OF LABOUR TO
CONTROLLED COMMUNICATION

Introducing a paragraph entitled 'The rôle of the hierarchy in the European process', H. Brugmans directly states: 'This is a short chapter. In fact there is no such role'.[13] Of course we cannot say that the hierarchical Church has directly contributed to the establishment of European organizations. The matter is less obvious in the area of opinions, especially in the structures of the Christian Democratic parties. But this statement does not take into account the mechanisms by which, since Pius XII's radio message in 1940, the Holy See has enjoyed a reinforced form of representation in communitarian institutions.[14]

The political aspect proper of the Church's action is so firmly pushed into another, unmentioned realm that, by some kind of elision, opposing political ideologies are metamorphized into 'heresies.' Then the Church becomes the partner of the Europeans against the 'nationalist heresy' which 'vaunts the spirit of the Gospel' . . . Later we read that 'Robert Schumann . . . was the John XXIII of politics'.[15] In this way the European idea becomes a religious ideal for the ideologues, even though this transformation obscures the network of influence operated by the hierarchy. By identifying themselves with religious orthodoxy, the European ideologues produce a form of legitimacy which more or less effectively masks their political interests. But for their part the religious ideologues draw, when speaking of Europe, on a new form of political efficacy, for it was on this ground of collective finalities that they were able to re-establish the conditions for the success of their message, even in the midst of the secularization process.[16]

Here I must recall my working hypothesis. The principle of the division of labour between Rome and the local churches consists in the following: the faithful have to see certain social practices as deriving with a certain necessity from the Christian message. But the churches are allotted only a portion each of this reproductive work, so that the political strategies of the hierarchy are parallel and independent. In one sense, the division into clergy and laity is reproduced at the level of relations between Rome and the European churches. The latter are engaged in the task of reflection on the pastoral aspects of European construction: morality, tourism, migration, and so on. Rome is concerned with direct action in the community institutions.

This is the essence of the argument put forward by the representative of the Secretariat of State in the face of the inclinations of the episcopal conferences to organize as a 'bureau' in relation to the community institutions. This is also the obvious intention of the structures determined by Rome.[17] For a sociological analysis, what is important here is the social relationship which structures communications between Rome and the western European churches. But this relationship clearly has as its objective function the cultivation of misunderstanding and alibis.

The core of the matter is certainly the double meaning which Rome gives to the term 'pastoral.' As we know, this work may serve to legitimize the Church's preoccupation with social institutions. In assuming control of the meaning of the word, Rome ensures its control of the division of labour in the Catholic Church. In fact, the representative of the Secretariat of State distinguishes and wishes to impose the distinction between a 'European pastoral problem' which consists in the harmonization of the structures of the churches (liturgy, catechesis, and so on) and 'the pastoral aspects of the activity of European institutions'. The first aspect requires exchanges of opinion between episcopal conferences, which will afford information on the decisions of the European communities. The other aspect arises from the unique competence of the Holy See, which alone has the formal rights to participate in the technical commissions and to obtain primary information on projects.[18] In these economic or legal questions which do not depend on the express competence of the Holy See, the present situation requires its representatives to consult documentation and to 'offer suggestions . . . through legitimate channels'. A service created by Rome makes sure that there is liaison work between the episcopal conferences and Rome. The pontifical representatives ensure 'an active though discreet presence of service and support for the efforts of the various states'.

Here we have all the elements of the problem. The division of labour between Rome and the western European churches results first in exclusion from communication of fully political practices and areas of influence. In making the discussion depend on the sole ground of religious identity,[19] political practices are dispensed with in favour of concrete realizations of orthodoxy. The relation that the local churches might enjoy with European affairs in their interrelations is limited to 'pastoral' or moral problems. Their field of negotiation is restricted to the Christian Democratic parties and excludes Socialist or regionalist movements and influences from orthopraxis. Finally, the local churches surrender their political responsibilities to the Holy See and look for compensation in the establishment of currents of opinion on the 'Teams of Hope' we hear of from the Belgian bishops. All the elements in question are interdependent.

CONCLUSION

My intention was to suggest a field of work which would reveal the core of the communication problem between Rome and the western European churches. In order to do so, I did not address myself to the content or even to the form of communications, but tried to show the objective social relationship which structured them. Having shown the full importance of the political setting in which these communications take place, I described the two levels of the division of labour which allow an answer to be given to the question: Who controls the subject-matter of the debate and way of debating it? I then proposed a working hypothesis for verification of documentation which is far too extensive to be treated adequately within the limits of an article.

Translated by John Griffiths

Notes

1. H. Brugmans, *Présence des Chrétiens sur le Chantier Européen* (Brussels, n.d.).

2. By this I mean political action by optimally institutionalized means. Cf., F. Houtart, in *Concilium*, 1974.

3. H. Brugmans, op. cit.; the second document is entitled, *La Vocation de l'Europe* (Brussels, 1976). This declaration is accompanied by an 'authorized commentary' entitled: *Construire l'Europe*. The third document is the *Compte Rendu de la Réunion des Représentants des Conférences Episcopales Européenes des Pays Membres de la Communauté Européene et du Conseil de l'Europe ainsi que de celles d'Espagne et du Portugal et des Représentants du Saint Siège* (Rome, 15 June 1976).

4. Mgr I. Cardinale, communication in *Compte Rendu*, p. 24.

5. Mgr G. Benelli, *Compte Rendu*, p. 4.

6. *Construire l'Europe*, pp. 3-4.

7. Cf., the lecture by Mgr Casaroli, 'The Holy See and the International Community' of which there is an Italian text in the *Osservatore Romano* (29 December 1974). See also the message of Pope Paul VI to the Council of Europe (28 January 1977) in *Osservatore Romano* (30 January 1977).

8. *La Vocation de l'Europe*, p. 6.

9. This mechanism is well analyzed by J. Matthes in 'Kirchliche Soziallehre als Wissenssytem', in *Internationale Dialog Zeitschrift*, II (1969), pp. 102-12. See also my comment on the document of the French bishops: 'Pour une Pratique Chrétienne de la Politique' (1972) in *Le Supplément* (Paris, no. 9, May 1974), pp. 199-253.

10. H. Brugmans, op. cit.

11. The author, a former professor at the Catholic University of Louvain, is a former rector of the Collège d'Europe in Bruges. His manifesto is accompanied by a 'postface' signed by fourteen European university teachers.

12. See also H. Brugmans, op. cit., pp. 22, 29.

13. Ibid., p. 8.

14. In the *Compte Rendu*, Mgr Benelli describes the history of this process since 1940. In 1948, Pope Pius XII sent a personal representative to the 'Congress of Europe' at the Hague. All the foundations of European institutions (Benelux, The Council of Europe, CECA, the Treaty of Rome, CEE, CEA) have been 'accompanied' by pontifical discourses. In 1962 the Holy See became a 'member in full right of the Council of Cultural Co-operation of the Council of Europe, then of the Committees for Higher Education, for Further Education, and for Cultural Development. In 1969-70 'the accreditation of a representative of the Holy See to the Council of Europe' was negotiated, and the accreditation was finalized in 1970. The Holy See was able to accredit a nuncio to the European Community. In 1973 he was a member of the Reestablishment Committee of the Council of Europe for refugees and excess populations in Europe. On 1 February 1974 the nuncio in France was appointed a special envoy to the Council of Europe (with delegate status). In March 1976 the Council of Ministers of the Council of Europe recognized the right of the Holy See to send observers to all the expert commissions. 'This statute', said Mgr Benelli, 'allows the Holy See to enjoy all the facilities open to member states'.

15. H. Brugmans, op. cit., pp. 13-14.

16. See my articles (with F. Dassetto): 'Le discour de partage', in *Lumen Vitae*, XXVIII (1973), No. 3, pp. 415-46, and 'Discours religieux et métamorphose des pratiques sociales', in *Social Compass*, XX (1973), pp. 389-403.

17. One might usefully compare the Roman strategy on European problems with the more general problem addressed by the *motu proprio Justiciam et Pacem* which lays down the definitive structures of the pontifical Justice and Peace Commission (10 December 1976), *Osservatore Romano* (17 December 1976).

18. Cf. *Compte Rendu*, pp. 5-8.

19. This is the area designated by one of the communications in the *Compte Rendu*, which is concerned with the question of the future moral quality of the European Community, threatened by 'the constant progress of Eurocommunism and Eurosocialism . . . which tends increasingly to de-Christianize European society with the constantly increasing support of militant agnosticism' (Mgr Cardinale, loc. cit., p. 15).

PART III

Communication between the Hierarchy and Lower Levels

Andrew M. Greeley

The Communal Catholic, the Two Churches: Fitting a Model

IN THIS ARTICLE I propose to discuss the implications for Catholicism in the United States of the development of 'voluntarism' in church affiliation. In particular, I shall focus in a concluding part of the article on voluntarism and problems of communication in the Church. By voluntarism in the present context I mean not merely that church membership is voluntary, there being no established Church and no real inheritance of religious affiliation (in this respect, American Catholicism has been voluntaristic since its very beginning); I mean a new kind of voluntarism. American Catholics have discovered not only that it is possible to be a Catholic or not to be a Catholic but that it is now possible to be a Catholic in the way one chooses to be a Catholic without regard to the 'official' norms of Catholic behaviour as these are imposed either by the teaching Church, through its hierarchal representatives, or by the élite, liberal Church, through bureaucratic agencies and journalistic media.

DEFINITION OF MODELS

In previous essays, I have used the model of 'communal Catholic'[1] and of the two Churches[2] to emphasize different aspects of this new voluntarism. The communal Catholic model suggests that many Catholics choose to be Catholics in the way in which Jews choose to be Jews: they identify with the Catholic community, are interested in the Catholic heritage and tradition, wish to pass on Catholicity to their children, but do not look to the Church for meaningful instructions on how to regulate their lives. Some communal Catholics are devout;

others are not; but the critical point is that even the undevout have no inclination to identify as anything else but Catholic, and even the devout have little inclination to yield much credibility to the Church as an official teacher.

The two-church model was proposed as an alternative to the two-church model of those who see one Church as the bureaucratic hierarchy and the other Church as the liberal laity. I contend that a much more useful model of the two Churches would compare the Church in the 'neighbourhoods' with the Church 'downtown'. The neighbourhood Church is the Church at the parish level and beneath; the downtown Church is the Church of the chancery office and above. Whether it is the Church of the conservative hierarchical bureaucracy *or* the Church of the liberal élites, the neighbourhood Church doesn't pay much attention to either. It asks only that the 'downtown' Church leave it alone, not hassle it, harass it, interfere with its work. It does not look to the hierarchical Church 'downtown' for guidance on birth control and it does not look to the liberal Church 'downtown' for guidance on radical attitudes or social problems. It pays little attention either to the *National Catholic Reporter* or the *Register;* to the *Commonweal* or to the *Sunday Visitor;* to the Washington and Chicago meetings of the bishops or to the Detroit meetings of the liberation theologians and the Call to Action. In fact, it is barely aware that these events exist.

Essential to both these models is the assumption that a substantial proportion of the Catholic population is no longer listening to communications from élite levels, whether those élite levels are hierarchical or liberal intellectual. In both cases, the rank-and-file Catholic either ignores or explicitly rejects the right of the élite to tell him what to do and how to live. Compliance with élite norms and directives, in other words, is part of the voluntary component of church affiliation. But the second assumption of both models is as critical as the first. The 'communal' Catholic and the 'neighbourhood' Catholic are free to affiliate or not affiliate, and to affiliate on terms of their own choosing, but by and large, continue to affiliate with little concern for the alleged inconsistency with which they are charged by the 'downtown' élites. The failure of communication, in other words, between 'downtown' and the 'neighbourhood' is so complete that the 'neighbourhood' not only no longer listens to 'downtown', but even denies *the right* of 'downtown' to establish norms.

DEAF EAR TO ÉLITES

In the present paper I intend to examine these two assumptions in the light of empirical data collected in the 1974 National Opinion Research study of the impact of Catholic schools,[3] and to ask what proportion of the Catholic laity reject the Church's right to teach them on both 'conservative' and 'liberal' matters, and what implication such rejection has for their religious practice.

A series of questions in the NORC study asked the respondent whether the Church had the right to teach 'what position Catholics should take on certain issues'. The two issues considered in this paper are racial integration and abortion. The answers to these two questions correlated at a sufficiently high level (.39), so that they can usefully be conformed into an index which is called the 'communal Catholic index.' Of the Catholics in the country, 85 per cent reject the Church's right to teach on one or the other of these two issues, and 49 per cent reject its right to teach on both of them. Half the Catholics in the United States, in other words, deny the Church has the right to lay down what position Catholics should take on 'proper means of family limitation' and 'racial integration'. The first of our two assumptions fits the data nicely: half the American Catholic population has turned off the 'downtown' Church on both the 'liberal' issue of racial integration and the 'conservative' issue of birth control.

What impact, then, does such a decision to reject the legitimacy of the Church's teaching have for these 'neighbourhood communal Catholics'? The first part of the answer is to inquire who the communal Catholics are, and how they differ from those who accept the Church's right to teach. In fact they are not very different from other Catholics. They are slightly younger (with a correlation of $-.13$) and slightly less likely to approve of ecclesiastical authority (modest negative correlations with the acceptance of papal fallibility, approval of Pope Paul's job performance, approval of bishop's job performance, and approval of the quality of sermons in their parish). But in other respects, the communal Catholics are not very different from anyone else. They are no more likely to be better educated, to have less or more Catholic education, to come from unreligious families; because they are as likely as others to have Catholic friends and to live in Catholic neighbourhoods. Nor is there any difference between men and women. The communal Catholics, in other words, are ever so slightly younger and somewhat more critical of the Church authority, but in other respects (including such variables as ethnicity, region of the country, size of dwelling, morale, psychological well-being, church contributions, marital status, which were also tested), there are virtually no differences between the communal Catholics and other Catholics.

The communal Catholics, then, seem to be no different from other Catholics save that they reject the Church's right to teach on abortion and on race. (For instance, they are not even significantly different in their *de facto* racial attitudes.) Has this decision to reject the official teaching of authority of the Church had much influence on their religious practice? Surely it would have been predicted beforehand that once one makes such a decisive break with an authoritative Church, one's traditional religious practice will be eroded, but, as we note in Table 2, there is virtually no evidence of such an erosion. Indeed, there are only two statistically significant differences between those who reject both the birth control and the racial integration teaching authority and the rest of the Catholic population. The communal Catholics are somewhat less likely to go to church two or three times a month or more—though 54 per cent of them still report that level of church attendance—and they are somewhat less likely to have attended a 'house liturgy' during the last two years (5 per cent for the communal Catholics; 8 per cent for all Catholics), but a quarter of the communal Catholics receive communion two or three times a month, more than half pray every day, more than three-quarters pray every week, more than three-quarters would support Catholic schools, more than half would give in excess of fifty dollars a year additional support to Catholic schools if asked to do so, 84 per cent have not thought of leaving the Church, one-fifth belong to parish organizations, more than a quarter have read a spiritual book in recent years, a fifth have participated in religious discussion groups, and a fifth have had serious conversations with a priest during the past two-year period. Neither in their background nor in their observable religious practice is there much difference between those Catholics who accept the teaching authority of the Church and those who reject it. However theologically and philosophically inconsistent it may be, a very substantial proportion of the Catholic population (about half) is able to reject ecclesiastical authority's right to teach authoritatively on race and on birth control and still maintain approximately the same levels of religious practice as do the general Catholic population.

CORROBORATING EVIDENCE

One suspects that this finding will be greeted with disbelief and perhaps contempt by the right-wing and left-wing élites. As one Roman cardinal said to me: 'It is too bad they don't have the faith any more'. And as a Pittsburgh monsignor said to me: 'We are ashamed of Catholics in the ethnic neighbourhoods'. Shameful and unfaithful they may be, but apparently they don't realize it. They reject the Church's right to teach on birth control and race and still continue their routine Catholic behaviour almost entirely unaffected by that rejection of teaching authority.

How can such inconsistency occur? First of all, one must note that there is no evidence at all that the people engaging in communal Catholic behaviour think that they're being inconsistent. They obviously do not think that it is necessary for devout Catholicism to accept the Church's right to teach authoritatively on racial and sexual matters. Élite Catholicism may say: 'But you have to accept our right to tell you what you should think about sex and/or race'. It is the essence of voluntarism that the communal Catholic can respond: 'That's what *you* say'. You have your official models of Catholic behaviour, in other words, and I have mine, and you can't make me live according to your model. Or, as one charming three-year-old of my acquaintance puts it: 'I don't gotta'.

There has been a substantial increase in the number of communal Catholics since the first NORC study in 1963 (rising from 30 per cent of the population to 50 per cent). As in most other matters reported in *Catholic Schools in a Declining Church,* virtually all the increase in the number of communal Catholics can be accounted for by a decline in support for papal authority and a decline in endorsement of the Church's official birth control teaching (and none of it relates to the support for the changes in the Second Vatican Council). My colleagues and I concluded in *Catholic Schools in a Declining Church* that the dramatic decline in Catholic religious practices seems to be affiliated with the birth control encyclical *Humanae Vitae* (there was considerable supporting evidence from other data sets for this conclusion). It now also appears that the fundamental explanation for the increase in the number of communal Catholics is the reaction of a large proportion of the Catholic population to *Humanae Vitae*—a reaction which seems to have brought both the left-wing and the right-wing élites off balance. The right-wing élites predicted that once the Pope had spoken, the matter would be closed, and Catholics would abandon artificial birth control. The left-wing élites predicted that once the Pope had spoken, Catholics would leave the Church and continue to practise birth control. In fact, both were wrong; Catholics continued to practise birth control and stayed in the Church (for the most part). The principal effects seem to be declining levels of religious devotion, and an increase in the number of those who reject the Church's right to be an authoritative teacher.

One should ponder for a moment the fact that three-quarters of those who reject the Church's right to teach authoritatively on race and on birth control are still willing to increase their annual contribution for the support of a *de facto* exercise of the Church's teaching function in the Catholic schools, and that half are willing to give fifty dollars and more a year to support the exercise of that function in their parish. It is all right, in other words, it would seem, for the Church to teach, but in certain areas of the exercise of the teaching authority, the Church no longer seems to enjoy any *credibility* as a teacher. The word credibility may be important here in the sense of 'believable'. One may speculate, in the absence of data, that a substantial number of Catholics in the United States simply do not think the Church is believable when it speaks on race or sex because it is their impression that the Church does not know what it's talking about; it does not understand the problems of marital intimacy and child rearing, it does not understand the problems of racially changing neighbourhoods, of urban crime, of deteriorating schools, inflation, increasing taxes and decline of governmental services. If people have made up their minds that you do not know what you're talking about, then you can talk until you are blue in the face and you will have no impact at all because they are not listening to you.

You can claim to speak for God, or alternatively, for the enlightened Christian conscience. The implicit response from the communal Catholic is that God knows what he's talking about but you don't and therefore I don't believe you're speaking for God. One may insist until Judgment Day that one is speaking for God, and if people deny that basic assumption, they will simply tune you out and turn you off.

So one has, then, in the American Church a major communication 'gap', a very substantial proportion of the laity, indistinguishable in most respects from the laity both in their origins and in their religious behaviour, who are simply no longer listening to the leadership, whether it be the leadership of the right or the left. They are not listening, it seems safe to speculate, because they don't find the leadership believable and do not believe the leadership's claim to speak for God or for the Gospel. It is not very likely that the communal Catholics will listen to the teaching authority on anything that has to do with either social problems or sex until the teaching authority becomes credible once again; that is to say, believable. If the speculation in this article is correct, believability was lost because those who officially or unofficially exercise the teaching function did not listen carefully enough to the problems of the ordinary people. The only solution would appear to be that the teaching authority, both official and unofficial, must begin again to listen once again to their problems. Instead of talking, instead of convening meetings, issuing statements, proclaiming calls to action, writing encyclicals, sending documents to the Holy Office, etc., etc., etc., the teaching authorities should start listening. The penalty for continued talk will be continued silence, if not the silence of empty halls, then at least the silence of those who are, with bored resignation, looking at their wrist watches wondering if the talk is ever going to end.

Notes

1. *The Communal Catholic* (New York, 1976).

2. 'Catholic Schools and the Two Churches: An Address to the National Catholic Educational Association'; given at the 74th Annual Convention and Religious Education Congress of the National Catholic Educational Association, San Francisco, California, 11-14 April, 1977.

3. Andrew M. Greeley, William C. McCready and Kathleen McCort, *Catholic Schools in a Declining Church* (Mission, Kansas, 1976).

TABLE 1

Correlations with 'Communal Catholic' Scale

Age	−.13
Education	*
Sex	*
Parents' religiousness	*
Spouse's religiousness	*
Papal infallibility	−.18
Approve of Pope Paul's job performance	−.15
Approve of bishop's job performance	−.12
Approve of pastor's job performance	*
Catholic friends	*
Catholic neighborhood	*
Approve of quality of sermons	−.18
Catholic education	*

* No statistically significant correlation.

(Scale made up of two items: rejection of Church's right to teach on birth control and on race.)

TABLE 2

*Differences Between Communal ** Catholics and All Catholics*

	Communal (per cent)	All (per cent)
Mass attendance (2 or 3 times a month)	54*	61
Communion reception (2 or 3 times a month)	27	32
Pray privately every day	54	60
Pray privately every week	77	80
Would give more to support Catholic schools	77	80
Would give more than fifty dollars a year	57	60
Serious conversation with priest in last 2 years	19	20
Has thought of leaving the Church (no)	84	85
Belongs to parish organization	19	21
Sympathy for resigned priests (a great deal)	33	32
Read a spiritual book in last 2 years	28	33
Participated in religious discussion group in last 2 years	19	21
Attended 'house liturgy' in last 2 years	5	8*

* Communal Catholics significantly different from *other* Catholics.
** Rejecting both birth control and racial teaching authority.

Janice Newson

Estranged Priests in Canada:
The Clerical Exodus Revisited

INTRODUCTION

THE RELATIONSHIP of the Second Vatican Council to recent developments in Catholicism has been the theme of many books, articles, and oral presentations. As the passage of time drives the Vatican II decade deeper into the pages of history, offering new vantage-points from which to reflect upon this era, no doubt more will be written and spoken on this theme.

Perhaps the single aspect of the era to most capture the attention of theologians and academicians alike has been the sharp increase in clerical resignations[1] following the Council. However, it could be argued that it is counter-productive to continue to focus on what may be viewed as a negative feature of post-Vatican II Catholicism, drawing attention from the consideration of issues relevant to the immediate and long-range future of the Christian Church.

Yet, there is reason to prolong the discussion of the clerical exodus in a journal which is to consider the theme of communication within the Church.

For, however else the Second Vatican Council is to be viewed—as a joyous celebration of the vitality of Catholic faith in the modern world, as a reaffirmation of the efficacy of Catholic institutions for coping with complex problems, as an attempt to reappraise, redefine or reunite—it must be recognized as one of the most significant efforts in ecclesiastical communication at least since the early Christians carried the Christian message throughout the Graeco-Roman Empire. If we are to criti-

57

cally evaluate communication within the Church, some energy must be given to considering how, if at all, and in what respects the subsequent increase in clerical disaffiliation was a response to this massive communication effort.

The purpose of this paper is to present a view of the post-conciliar exodus based on a study conducted by this writer of a large urban diocese in Canada. In addition, perspectives offered in other studies of this subject, conducted by social scientists using North American data, will be reviewed. The discussion will focus not so much on the statistical evidence provided by these studies, since such evidence may have little validity in regions of the Church which differ significantly from the North American examples, but rather on their interpretations of the relationship between the Second Vatican Council and the subsequent increase in clerical resignations.

SEARCHING FOR EXPLANATIONS

The ink was barely dry on the Vatican II documents when indications of a 'crisis in the priesthood' began to dominate, if not dampen the enthusiasm of post-conciliar discussions. However, the concern that priestly work and life was being seriously affected by complex changes in patterns of religious behaviour did not originate with the post-conciliar eruptions. Before the Council, Joseph Fichter, among others, argued that factors such as the increased social and geographical mobility of lay populations in urban environments created serious dilemmas in the organization of clerical functions. He suggested, albeit cautiously, that changes in the traditional approach to priestly work might be necessary for the Church to achieve its sacred mission in the modern world and for members of the priesthood to effectively conduct their spiritual ministry.[2]

In many respects, the problems identified by Fichter and others are similar to those considered in literature on the Protestant ministry.[3] Kenneth Thompson's analysis of societal changes which affected the Church of England throughout the nineteenth and twentieth centuries drew the same conclusions regarding the increased rôle strain of the Anglican parish minister in the urban context.[4]

It is reasonable to argue, then, that the increase in resignations from the priesthood reflected a trend already underway in many other religious communities, a trend whose sources were rooted in transformations in the social and cultural life of modern societies and in problems associated with the nature of the institutional framework encompassing clerical work and life. This argument implies that the sudden increase in resignation decisions followed quite coincidentally the adjournment

of the Second Vatican Council. That is, the Council had little, if anything, to do with the crisis except, perhaps, in failing to implement
changes in institutional practices which would have alleviated the tensions associated with the clerical rôle.

Following this line of reasoning, some investigations of the post-
conciliar crisis have identified specific features in the changing societal
milieu and in the organization of clerical work which create problems,
conflicts, and diminished job satisfaction in the priesthood and hence,
which underlie resignation decisions. For example, Hall and Schneider
attempted to isolate 'organizational climate' characteristics contributing to various levels of job satisfaction in the priesthood. Although the
study did not focus on resigned priests, an analysis of active priests
who resigned after being interviewed for the study was used to support
the conclusion that resignations are associated with work setting
and career characteristics which produce low levels of job-satisfac-
tion.[5]

Evidence such as this supports the view that the changing complex-
ion of modern society and the traditional pattern of work organization
in Catholic institutions have created serious problems for the clergy.
However, if it is assumed that these problems are, in themselves, the
underlying cause of resignation, why did this particular symptom of
discontent, so sudden and dramatic in its appearance, not emerge until
the mid to late nineteen-sixties?

One answer to this question is to point out that resigning from the
priesthood, which may have been more difficult in the past for a
Catholic priest than for a Protestant minister, was made easier by the
climate of activism and departure from tradition which generally
characterized this decade. Even so, a number of questions remain
unanswered and many specific dimensions of the Catholic experience
of disaffiliation are left unexplained.

For example, were all members of the priesthood exposed equally to
the problems underlying discontent and, if not, why not? If all priests
were equally exposed to these problems, why did only some priests
resign? Was resignation the only response to difficulties? If the Council
was not associated with the resignation trend, why did interpretations
of Council documents and the struggle over their implementation figure
so strongly in justifications given for resigning?

Other investigations of the clerical unrest following the Council have
adopted the view that the Council, itself, had some relationship to the
subsequent resignation increase although the precise nature of this
relationship has not been fully explored in discussions to date.

A common view of the relationship portrays the Council as creating
or accentuating a cleavage within the Catholic community which

polarized those who wished to preserve traditional practices against those who carried the banners of *aggiornamento* from the Council's chambers into local Church institutions. A refined version of this portrayal views the Council as emphasizing renewed definitions of Christian ministry which were incompatible with the established ecclesiastical structures. In failing or refusing to implement the organizational changes necessary for accomplishing renewed ministries, the Council inevitably thrust into the local Church arena the difficulties arising from this incompatibility.

Following this argument, the resignation trend has been presented as a consequence of the struggle to implement, in the face of entrenched traditionalism, the renewal thrusts of the Council documents. Resigning priests are depicted as advocates of the renewal spirit who adopted values and perspectives on their ministries which conflicted with the traditional demands and expectations of priestly work and life.

For example, a study by Schallert and Kelley describes the clerical drop-out as 'an individual who has been deeply affected by the spirit of the Second Vatican Council . . . strongly oriented toward change . . . (and who) defines the Church as unchanging'.[6] Greeley and Schoenherr's analysis of the responses of a subsample of priests who stated an intention to resign designates 'modern values' and 'desire to marry' as two major causal factors leading to resignation.[7]

Yet these explanations of resignation decisions are not entirely convincing, particularly in view of the fact that some of the investigators, themselves outspoken advocates of renewal, are also active members of the priesthood. Hence, while the evidence indicates that many resigning priests were advocates of reform, it cannot be argued conversely that nonresigning priests were *not* advocates of reform. What, then, distinguished the priest who resigned from the priest who did not resign when both advocated renewal?

EMPIRICAL STUDY OF A LARGE DIOCESE

This writer's study of the post-conciliar exodus,[8] in focusing on the dynamics of the change process more than on identifying the stances toward renewal adopted by various segments of the Catholic community, develops a perspective which answers some of the questions raised in the course of this discussion.

The analysis (based on a matched sample of resigned and active priests) suggests, firstly, that while many sources of clerical discontent were related to societal and institutional factors which pre-dated the Vatican II era, the Council's stress on renewal precipitated and accentuated, in the post-conciliar period, a growing awareness of tensions in the priest rôle. That is, the struggle over implementing the Council's directives aggravated many of these tensions while, at the same time, the language of renewal provided an acceptable basis for interpreting these problems and for developing a broadly based, comprehensive critique of the ecclesiastical structures which traditionally encompassed priestly work and life.

Second, neither resigned priests nor active priests adopted uniform attitudes toward renewal itself. Some resigned priests became frustrated with the institutional and attitudinal resistance to reform; some felt, insofar as the Council had supported renewal at all, that the Church had betrayed its commitment to an orthodox Catholic faith; others had become disillusioned that the Church could not manage a dignified, unchaotic, and peaceful transition if such was needed. Some active priests were deeply committed to and actively pursuing the path of renewal, others were concerned with the preservation of traditional Catholic practices, while others are best characterized as having been uninterested in either side of the renewal issue.

Since attitudes toward renewal did not, in themselves, clearly distinguish resigned from active priests, the major concern of this study was to consider how and on what basis members of the priesthood became engaged in the actual dynamics of the change process, and how this engagement affected their continuation in the clerical vocation. Although all conclusions of this analysis cannot be reported here, some important points will be made.

Priests' engagement in the process of change was shaped, to a large degree, by their own career development. For example, priests whose ordination was very recent, having been in the seminary during all or part of the conciliar period, were more aware of the substance of conciliar discussions and of the theology of renewal which underscored the conciliar documents than the majority of priests engaged in full-time ministries during this same period. Yet these priests, often lacking experience in the actual functioning of church institutions and having little influence over decision making, had available to them far less than their older, experienced colleagues, the resources needed for managing relationships which inevitably affected the quality of their own ministry, such as relationships to superiors, co-workers, and members of the lay community. Hence, they were especially vulnerable to becoming frustrated with the complexities and slowness of change and frequently adopted responses to these difficulties which, in the post-conciliar context, alienated them from these crucial relationships and, in many cases, from the clerical rôle itself.

Some experienced priests, however, whose career development anticipated promotion in the near future, were affected in a different way by the change process. Even under normal circumstances, as these priests became increasingly impatient for the opportunity 'to be in charge' and to have more responsibility, their vocational satisfaction tended to decline. In post-conciliar conditions, chaotic and confusing in many respects, their impatience was supported by the general criticism of traditional practices, such as the lengthy period of apprenticeship with senior colleagues. Remaining in the priesthood often depended upon the timing of the promotion, and resignation decisions were sometimes triggered by the out of turn appointment of a younger priest as pastor or director of an attractive 'experimental' programme.

The engagement of priests in the process of change was also shaped by the strategy for implementing renewal adopted by the local church hierarchy.

For example, the leadership of the diocese under study favoured a controlled approach to renewal, publicly designating certain parishes and special ministries as 'experiments' in change rather than encouraging renewal practices to emerge spontaneously throughout the diocese. On the one hand, priests assigned to these programmes were encouraged, indeed instructed by their superiors to pursue renewal ministries while, on the other hand, being critically scrutinized by segments of the lay and clerical communities who were unsympathetic to specific changes. Furthermore, the church leaders who had encouraged these efforts in the first instance, often withdrew their support when the innovations began to create serious divisions within the local church community or when the changes extended beyond anticipated boundaries.

By contrast, some priests, under less exposed conditions and removed from the special supervision of the local hierarchy, could proceed with renewal efforts without becoming entangled in widespread controversy.

The problems created for some priests by this policy were compounded by the fact that some priests who tended to be selected for these innovative programmes were often unprepared to deal with the consequences. For, since the experimental programmes were considered vital to local renewal efforts, they were often staffed by priests who, in their previous career development, had been considered the most promising members of the local clerical contingent, had received prestigious assignments or responsible positions earlier than usual, and had been held in high favour by the local leadership. However, in the experimental context these men often found themselves in the unusual position of being criticized and attacked by local pastors as well as by other priests and members of the lay community and of being out of favour with the very same superiors who had previously sponsored their success.

In contrast, some priests who had been engaged in ministries considered relatively marginal to the Church's concerns in the pre-conciliar period became more highly esteemed in the post-conciliar period because the revised ranking of ministry priorities, implied in the emphases of the conciliar documents, brought new recognition of the value of their work.

The examples provided above illustrate some of the ways in which priests were affected by the dynamics of the change process. Resignation was only one of the options adopted by priests in response to these situations and it was adopted for several different reasons. Some priests, traumatized to some extent by their experiences, were vulnerable to incidents which triggered a resignation decision, such as an intense confrontation with a superior, becoming more than casually involved with a woman, or being removed from an important assignment. Other priests found their personal and vocational commitments so transformed by their involvement in renewal activities that the priesthood was no longer seen as a suitable channel for expressing these commitments. Others resigned simply because the option was now available, having been made more acceptable by the fact of other resignations.

CONCLUSION

What, then, is to be learned from the Church's experiences of this period?

First, the analysis presented here implies that little could have been done to prevent entirely the clerical exodus, unless, of course, the renewal path had never been supported by the Council. Even so, writers such as Greeley argue, and I agree, that the crisis would have emerged eventually, though perhaps more slowly and gradually.[9]

Secondly, the analysis reveals a certain naiveté in the Church about the ease with which change could be accomplished and a lack of awareness of how renewal efforts would be affected by the Church's own history. The style of leadership provided and the nature of the commitments which priests carried with them, even while engaged in renewal efforts, was inevitably marked by traditional upbringing, traditional training, and experiences in traditional institutions.

That this was the case is not the point. The point is that the conflict and confusion resulting from the decision to adopt the renewal path should have been anticipated. More support than was given should have been available for those who became frustrated, even belligerent; patience should have been shown to those who could not understand and more wisdom should have been used in placing members of the clergy into the centre of the controversy.

What is regrettable is not that some priests resigned, but rather that the reference to 'estrangement' in the title of this paper applies not only to the resignees but to many priests who lived through this period. For indeed, while resigned priests often found themselves alienated from the lay and clerical community which criticized their efforts, or from superiors who withdrew support, or from the council Fathers who endorsed renewal, so active priests often became alienated from those who left, feeling, perhaps, that enough effort had not yet been given, that change had been expected to come too quickly, or that the initial commitment to the vocation had not been strong enough to endure 'the worst of times'.

Notes

1. This paper will be concerned only with the resignations from the ordained priesthood.

2. See J. Fichter, *Social Relations in the Urban Parish* (Chicago, 1954).

3. For example, Samuel Blizzard's noted articles are often used as a starting point for studies of both the Catholic and Protestant ministry. For example, see S. Blizzard, 'The Minister's Dilemma', in *Christian Century,* vol. 73 (1956), pp. 508-10; idem, 'The Parish Minister's Integrating Roles', in *Religious Education,* vol. 53 (1958), pp. 374-80.

4. K. Thompson, *Bureaucracy and Church Reform* (Oxford, 1970), pp. 230-32.

5. D. Hall & B. Schneider, *Organizational Climates and Careers* (New York, 1973), pp. 157-59.

6. E. Schallert & J. Kelley, 'Some Factors Associated with Voluntary Withdrawal from the Priesthood', in *Lumen Gentium,* vol. 25 (1970), p. 459.

7. R. Schoenherr & A. Greeley, 'Role Commitment Processes and the American Priesthood', in *American Sociological Review,* vol. 39 (1974), pp. 407-26.

8. Janice A. Newson, 'The Roman Catholic Clerical Exodus: A study of rôle-adaptation and organizational change' (unpublished Ph.D. dissertation, University of Toronto, Toronto, 1976).

9. A. Greeley, *Priests in the United States* (Garden City, New York, 1972), pp. 19-29.

Giovanni Cereti

Divorce in Italy

THE DIVORCE REFERENDUM AND ITS HISTORICAL CONTEXT

WE NEED to go quite far back to understand the full significance of the divorce referendum in Italy. We must remember, for example, that the Italian people did not experience the crisis of conscience of the Reformation, which certainly helped to increase the individual believer's sense of personal responsibility in the countries concerned. They were also largely unaffected by the other great growth crisis constituted by the French Revolution. On the other hand, they experienced the Counter-Reformation and the Restoration, and have long been dominated by a culture cut off from the modern world, whose typical products are *Mirari Vos* and the *Syllabus*. The hierarchical view of the Church pronouncing 'from above' expressed in such documents helps to explain why the Italian people, in whom individual self-awareness made such great strides towards freedom during the Middle Ages, and who were at the forefront of human development, at least in economic, cultural and artistic matters in the fifteenth century, were willing to accept submission and so great a surrender of their private judgment to the authority of the Catholic Church, not only in spiritual and moral matters but in politics.

Illuminism, the bourgeois revolution, capitalist development and the unification of Italy itself took place partly in opposition to the Church, but the great mass of the people remained outside or at least passive in the face of these movements. Socialism was more widely diffused among the masses but it never succeeded in overcoming the influence of the Church, except in very limited areas. At the end of the last century and the beginning of this, in the split between the 'legal country' and the 'real country',[1] the Church could rightly boast that the 'real country', that is the majority of Italians, was with it, even though for various reasons it had not yet achieved political expression.

With the solution of the Roman question and the great papal figures of this century, the Church regained a strong influence also in public life, although today when speaking of the relations between the Church and Fascism we tend to call it 'co-existence' rather than 'connivance'. Because it stood in as mediator, especially in the North at the end of the war, the Church hierarchy realized, once democracy was restored and after a period of uncertainty, that it could still hold influence, particularly in the struggle against Communism, by using the tools of democracy. Hence its support of the Christian Democratic party, which gained an absolute majority in 1948 and has remained in power ever since, sometimes with the support of other smaller parties.

The authority of the Church, confirmed by the presence of a strong Catholic party and by its own new self-awareness during the Pope John and Vatican Council period, was able to withdraw from Italian politics.

But this progressive withdrawal was threatened by law 1/XII/1970, which introduced the possibility of civil divorce in Italy and was approved by a coalition of parties from the Liberal to the Communist. At first it was mainly part of the organized Catholic laity which felt obliged to intervene, appealing once more to the 'real country' as opposed to the 'legal'. They quickly collected a million-and-a-half signatures asking for a referendum on the repeal of the law. After various postponements and the failure or refusal of the possibilities offered for avoiding an electoral clash, the referendum was fixed for 12 May, 1974. Most of the Italian bishops had not really wanted it; they took it for granted that a Catholic could not accept a civil law permitting divorce and allowed themselves to become involved in the fight without sufficient deliberation or consultation with the people. The results of the referendum constituted the first occasion on which the authority of the Church, which had been stripped of temporal power a century before but still felt secure in the support of the majority of the Italian people, found itself in the minority. The Italian people had given a different judgment from the hierarchy's. What had happened? Had Italians renounced the Church? Had they apostasized from the faith *en masse?* Pope and bishops, whose information had been inaccurate and were therefore surprised by the results, fretted for the answer to these questions.

THE DEVELOPMENT OF ITALIAN SOCIETY OVER THE LAST THIRTY YEARS

One very significant factor can help us to understand the results of the referendum. It was the towns that gave the victory to the pro-divorce side. As compared with the election results of the pro-divorce parties, the pro-divorce votes at the referendum increased by only 2% in the country but by 19% in the towns. As compared with the election results of the anti-divorce parties, the anti-divorce vote dropped by 30% in the big cities (this figure of votes lost includes spoilt ballots and abstentions). Socio-cultural factors to do with urban culture seem therefore to have prevailed over the strictly political and party loyalty.[2]

The recent growth in the urban population can be summed up by giving a few significant figures. In 1951 agricultural workers were 42% of the active population, but only 17% in 1971. During the same period industrial workers increased by two million and workers in the tertiary sector by two million and a half. The country and mountain villages were being depopulated and the cities growing accordingly, with all the cultural phenomena attendant upon such a change.

The Church's organizational and cultural structures failed to keep up. In 1951 more than 50% of parishes had less than a thousand inhabitants. These were mainly rural parishes in which 12% of the Italian population lived. In 1966 the number of parishes with less than a thousand inhabitants had increased, whereas the total population in this sector had grown smaller. The disproportionate staffing of the country is immediately apparent, especially when we realise that in many dioceses the young and vigorous priests are often confined to tiny mountain or country parishes and only promoted to large urban parishes when they get old. Thus the influence of the church, which is still strong in rural areas, where the population is declining, dwindles dramatically in the towns, particularly in the newly-built suburbs. This can be inferred from all the indicators of religious behaviour, from religious practise to membership of Catholic associations. The number of nuns is still large but they are largely concerned with works of mercy or marginal activities which have practically no cultural or political weight. Most of the priests come from the country, and with their education and life-style they are not well trained to cope with the mentality and culture of modern urban society. Even four-fifths of the bishops are of rural origin and live in episcopal seats twenty-five percent of which are still situated today in places with less than 20,000 inhabitants, and 15% of which with less than 10,000.

RURAL AND URBAN MENTALITY: TWO OPPOSING CULTURES

The above-mentioned data are also important because rural and urban society have different outlooks.[3]

A traditional-type rural society's world view is archaic, governed by a set of static and immutable laws, in which wisdom, regarded chiefly as experience, is passed on from generation to generation, and authority is still given heavy weight. In this view, which is resistant to change, marriage and family remain an especially sacred reality: the institution is more important than the people concerned, and the duty to give life to the next generation, to carry on the patriarchal family, is more important than personal fulfilment in marriage. In this context a law allowing divorce is like a desecration and appears to open the way to the total ruin of society.

The world-view characteristic of urban society is more dynamic. Permanent faithful marriage is a goal to be striven for, and is primarily concerned with the happiness and personal fulfilment of the marriage partners themselves. There is much greater trust in personal conscience, the law becomes relative and given at most a pedagogical function.

In urban society literacy is higher and there is a chain effect of a whole series of factors and information media which gradually substitute self-motivation for the acceptance of authority on how to behave. On the other hand, authority is still important in the country and the priest can still exert a strong influence on behaviour.

THE REFERENDUM: A TEST OF THE COMMUNICATION DIFFICULTIES BETWEEN THE TWO CULTURES IN THE CHURCH

The structure of the Italian Church and the difference in mentality and language between the two cultures described above largely explain the communication difficulties there have been in Italy between the hierarchy and those of the clergy and laity who are in closer contact with the rest of the population. These difficulties, which became particularly obvious from 1967 on with the growth of grass-roots communities and the spread of 'dissent', were revealed most clearly in the referendum.

Because of their social origins and education, the bishops were thinking of a static world view characteristic of rural society. They were unaccustomed to listening to other people's views, to dialogue; they were trained by an old-fashioned ecclesiology to hold that divine assistance is given directly to the clergy alone and that the faithful have only to listen and obey, and thus they were incapable of grasping the cultural change that had occurred in society and in the Catholic laity itself. They had few contacts with the outside world and the few they had were filtered by a circle of faithful ecclesiastics afraid of conveying news that would be unwelcome, or by timid and mostly conservative laity. They were cut off from the daily exchanges which arise from walking about among ordinary people, taking the bus like everybody else or going to the cinema, and thus the bishops were deprived of all those many channels of communication, not just verbal ones, that ordinary people have and which form an important part of the structure of communication existing within a society. The warnings that influential lay and ecclesiastical journalists constantly reiterated to the hierarchy through the press on the 'risks' of the referendum, also went unheard. It was as if they were not aware of the direction gradually being taken by part of the clergy and Catholic laity, who had raised a constant stream of questions and discussions after the approval of the law on divorce. Wasn't it necessary to distinguish more clearly between the requirement of faith on the absolute indissolubility of marriage and the need to advance on the political and legislative level, which concerned everybody whether Catholic or no? Why had not Catholics in other countries ever thought it necessary to conduct such a desperate struggle against civil legislation allowing divorce? In the case where a marriage had in fact broken down, couldn't the possibility of civil divorce and the creation of a new union recognised by law be considered a lesser evil? Should the nullity procedures and approved dispensations in ecclesiastical courts, which by virtue of the Concordat also had civil jurisdiction in Italy, really be considered as the ideal solution to the problem of broken marriages? And above all, after Vatican II and the declaration on religious liberty, wasn't it necessary to respect what many regarded as a due recognition of the conscientious rights of religious and political minorities? And finally wasn't it necessary to oppose a regressive move of the Right, which was what seemed to have been the decisive factor in certain sectors of the Christian Democrat party in setting up the referendum?[4]

The answer given to these questions caused a new agreement to emerge among Italian Catholics on the moral duty (Att 5.29) not to vote for the repeal of the divorce law. The creation of the 'League of Democratic Catholics' formalized this agreement and gave it widespread publicity. The position taken by this sector of Italian Catholicism made it possible to prevent the referendum battle becoming a straight fight between Catholics and non-Catholics. The battleground shifted to within the Italian Church; this brought out clearly the cultural difference, which was also partly a religious difference, between two sectors of Italian Catholicism and the lack of communication between the episcopate in particular and a large number of the people of God.

There was a lack of communication upwards, as could be seen from the hierarchy's inability to grasp the reasons why the most advanced sector of the Italian Church had chosen to keep the divorce law, and to understand the way the majority were thinking. This was why the hierarchy was surprised by the referendum results, which they could have foreseen more easily if they had been in closer contact with the people.

There was also a lack of communication downwards: the bishops failed to convey their message to the great mass of the population, either because the language they used had become unintelligible in the new urban culture, or because the parish clergy refused to pass it on.[5] The drastic steps taken shortly before the polls, and in particular the suspension of Dom Franzoni *a divinis,* had the opposite effect to that the hierarchy intended.[6] On the conscious level, these steps were intended to act as a warning but on the unconscious level they worked to the contrary. Many floaters who might have been persuaded to support the hierarchy's position by a calm and respectful approach reacted strongly against what they considered to be intolerant bullying and an undue use of spiritual means in a political question, which was going against the principles of freedom of conscience laid down by Vatican II.

FROM AN ECCLESIOLOGY 'DOWNWARDS' TO AN ECCLESIOLOGY OF COMMUNION

The choices made at the referendum did not of course mean that the majority of the Italian people renounced their faith and abandoned communion with the Church. The people had merely shown that they had reached a new maturity and ability to 'judge for themselves' (Lk 12:57) in social and ethical matters. They also showed that Catholic life today was conducted with more respect for the rights and opinions of others, with more care not to confuse political and more properly spiritual matters and that at the same time democracy had been fully accepted, with all its implications of pluralism, tolerance, separation of spheres of jurisdiction and the secularity of the state. Thus the strongest test case of the poor communication within the Italian Church became an inducement to review the situation and to try to do something to improve communication. In recent years the hierarchy had in fact moderated its attitude, as was shown for example in the convention of November 1976 on 'Evangelization and Human Promotion', which spoke of the need to listen better and pay more attention to other people's views, to be less cut off and to take more part in everyday life. The Italian episcopate is gradually realising that no decision can be taken today without being subject to debate and dialogue and making clear the reasons on which their decisions are based. The 'downwards' hierarchical ecclesiology is slowly making way for an ecclesiology of communion. The separation between clergy and laity is becoming less rigid, through the creation of numerous community movements, in which faith is rediscovered more authentically and *koinonia* (community) becomes a reality involving clergy and laity. This new growth of community is a hopeful sign that soon the painful negative survivals from the past will be outgrown, integrism will be progressively abandoned, and the rents in the robe which is the Italian Church will be mended. A new consensus is emerging based on human values and a new style of life in the Church, centred upon the hearing of the word of God, the eucharist and service. This is very hopeful for the people of God in Italy.

Notes

1. Cf. for example, Anonimo's arguments in 'Il Parlamento italiano nel 1861, I, il regno della maggioranza', in *Civilita Cattolica* IV, IX (1861), pp. 513-30; 'II, il regno della minoranza', X, pp. 33-47.

2. This analysis is based mainly on A. Parisi: 'Questione cattolica e referendum: l'inizio di una fine' in *Il Mulino* 233 (1974), pp. 410-38, which also gives more precise references for some of the data quoted in this paragraph. Certainly other factors were also involved: the relationship between North and South, the influence of the party machines, and in particular the efficiency of the Communist party machine and the inefficiency of the Christian Democrats, and so on. I have no space here to analyze these factors.

3. This phenomenon is not of course only Italian. L. Roussel, *Le mariage dans la societé française contemporaine* (Paris, 1975), has shown that divorce by law is more readily accepted by the young, people living in cities (particularly in the Paris region), and the better educated. Especially significant is the fact that in the provinces divorce by mutual consent is accepted by 47% of non-Catholics and only 6% of Catholics, whereas in Paris the religious variable ceases to count.

4. Cf. G. Zizola, in *Concilium* 10 (1974).

5. 'The hierarchy whose dark power is the more feared the less it is visible, has not even succeeded (or at least only minimally) in conveying its own appeal. Asked shortly before the referendum about the ''sources'' from which they had received messages on the subject under discussion, only 12.8% of those interviewed by Demoskopea said they had heard it spoken about by ''the parish priest in church or by the priest''. Thus among eight ''sources'' the priest came next to last, with only trade-union representatives below, with the small difference that, whereas the trade unions had assumed a neutral stance, the Church had taken a very firm position' (Parisi, art. cit., note 2, p. 425). Among those who went to church every Sunday, the percentage rose only to 22.6%.

6. We have proof of the enormous gap between the Italian episcopate and at least certain categories of young people and university students in the research

of M. I. Macioti, 'Chiesa CEI Franzoni: per una ipostesi di analisis contestuale degli attegiamenti', in *La Critica Sociologica,* 33-4 (1975), pp. 197-227. According to this survey, conducted by means of a listing of attributes, for the sample of the population interviewed, ex-Abbot Franzoni was 'democratic, sincere, altruistic, objective, poor, modest'; *viz.* all positive qualities with the only negative one being 'disobedient'. On the other hand, both the Church in general and the Italian Episcopal Conference in particular were called 'authoritarian, unacceptable, corrupt, conservative, factious, irreligious, dirty, anti-democratic, intolerant, mixed up in politics: all negative attributes, the only positive one being strong', which, in the case of the Church is of course ambivalent. Although the lack of rigour in the selection of the sample unfortunately· detracts from the reliability of the results, it certainly gives us cause for reflection on the image that some sectors of the population, particularly the young, have of church authorities.

Ed Grace

The Catholic Left in Italy

THE CONTEMPORARY lack of a Catholic left-wing party in Italy does not mean that there are no Italian Catholics on the Left. On the contrary, today, there are more than ever before. It is difficult to be exact but, judging conservatively from recent events and statistics, it is not a question of hundreds of thousands but of millions. At the very least five million Catholics who go to mass with some regularity voted on 20 June 1976 for Marxist-inspired parties; an estimated 25% of these would probably identify themselves as 'Catholic' and 'Communist' or 'Socialist'.[1] Many are active members of their parishes and of their respective parties; some of these identifiable Catholics are even members of the central committees of their parties. This mass of Catholics have made this choice, notwithstanding the excommunication in 1949 and the most recent urgings of the hierarchy and the pope himself not to do so.

The motivations behind their voting for these parties (instead of the Christian Democratic Party, the so-called 'Catholic' party, indicated as being obligatory in conscience) rely on a series of interwoven factors ranging (a) from the present economic crisis combined with the negative socio-administrative results of thirty years of Catholic party government to the socio-ideological dynamics unleashed by the student-worker upheaval of 1968-69; (b) from the non-dogmatic policies of the Communist and Socialist parties to the documents of Vatican II on freedom of conscience and political liberty; (c) from the continual growth of Catholic dissent, especially after 1966, against a pre-Vatican II restoration process which began to penetrate many sectors of the Italian Church to the explosion of Christians for Socialism on to the scene in 1972; and (d) from the decades of long patient work of practising Catholic-Communists to the psychological influence of the public support of some of Italy's leading Catholic laymen for the Communist party in the 1976 elections.

The complex measurement of the interrelation of these, and still other, factors of what seems like mass religious disobedience is beyond the possibilities of this article. Nevertheless, a synthesis of the theoretical differences is helpful in searching for future ground for dialogue between the Catholic Left and the hierarchy. Italian left-wing Catholics maintain that neither specific, historical Christian social programmes nor a Catholic party can be deduced from the Gospel or from Catholic dogma. Moreover, their membership of non-dogmatic, Marxist parties cannot be said to contradict the Gospel or Catholic tradition, because that choice, they state, is *not deduced* from their religious beliefs but is based upon reason and their historical search to realize the gospel call to all generations to bring about justice. On the other hand, the hierarchy as a whole maintains that belonging to, or at least voting for, the Catholic party is a matter of being a good Catholic and that specific forms of Catholic social programmes—not just principles of 'justice', 'equality', 'common good', and so on—can be deduced from the Gospel and/or from Catholic tradition.

In short, these two positions seem to exclude what might be called 'grounds' for formal dialogue. Nevertheless, left-wing Catholics carry on informal, unofficial dialogue on *all* levels within the Church.

On analyzing the massiveness and the complexity of this phenomenon in Italy today, two fundamental factors emerge: *(a)* The solid theoretical convictions of left-wing Catholics that they can be good Catholics and members of left-wing parties. *(b)* The position of Italian left-wing parties in regard to religion. Important aspects of both these factors have their origins deep in Italian history, one of the most pertinent periods of which was 1941-45. Then, long before Marxist-Christian dialogue, Italian Catholics had already founded a 'Christian-Communist Party'. If we concentrate on this period, the contemporary phenomenon becomes less surprising and more profound in all its pastoral-theological significance.

CATHOLIC ANTI-FASCISTS

As far back as 1937, spontaneous anti-Fascist Catholic groups had been founded in Rome. These groups were made up primarily of young men whose principal characteristics were that they were practising Catholics, active in their parishes and almost all members of Catholic Action. The majority also had contact with the more moderate sectors of Catholicism and were esteemed both by their local pastors as well as certain sectors of the Vatican.[2]

At that time, the most pressing problem of these future founders of the Catholic-Left parties was how to draw other Catholics into the actual struggle to overthrow Fascism in 1937. A document circulated clandestinely by one such group outlined their aims: 'clandestine struggle with all its means and risks (jail, etc.) alone can save Catholics from serious responsibilities for racism and war' and 'to destroy the myth of the political unity of all Catholics, exploited and exploiters, and to promote a left-wing Christian movement'.[3]

From this small beginning, practice, reflection and theory led to a recognition of the validity of historical materialism. This qualitative jump was in 1941 when these various Catholic anti-Fascist groups founded a new organization, the Unifying[4] Cooperative Party (UCP).[5]

In their extensive manifesto they defended Catholicism as 'still having many things to say to humanity as the gospel teachings are inexhaustible.' But, they argued, Catholics 'can only be heard if every residue of conservatism and prudence is overcome' and they warned of 'the reactionary spirit, fed by those who see the priest as the defender of the *status quo*'.

On the other hand, while these Catholics expressed their willingness to form an alliance with the Italian Communist Party (ICP) they also called for the 'suspension of anti-religious propaganda' and the anti-clericalism which they described as 'a classical infantile disease of Communism'. They argued, as Marxists, that 'clearing the ground of these ahistorical prejudices' was 'a very important and revolutionary gesture'.

The manifesto also held that the social dimensions of freedom, religion, education, and so on were 'goods ontologically superior to the economic good'. This position was taken in order to 'safeguard the human person' (a religious value for them) and 'to free man from the superstructures of the Leninistic state'.[6]

As the war grew more bitter, towards the end of 1942 the UCP decided to take a more clear-cut class position and changed its name to the Christian-Communist Party (CCP). This phase was short-lived as about four hundred members were arrested in Rome in May 1943. In the period from their imprisonment through their release in July 1943 (the Italian armistice), to German occupation and renewed clandestine action, they changed from a party (CCP) into a movement, the Christian Communist Movement (CCM). In the meantime they had seen that the only real distinction between them and the ICP was philosophico-religious (the ICP then required philosophical adherence for membership), and that religion alone was an insufficient base for a party.

In April-May 1944, still under the German occupation, the Christian Communist Movement presented a more systematic exposition of their position in a booklet entitled *Communism and Catholics*. 'Christian Doctrine is not history', they stated, trying to establish the relationship between religion and politics. 'It is a meta-historical fact of revelation, which man did not make, but received. The progress of human civilization cannot change it; it must, however, in some way be rendered true in history so that its light does not remain distant and inoperative'. For them, the historical task of religion was 'to indicate the moral ends of man, that is, the ultimate scope of the human person'. The end which religion proposed to political activity was to 'promote the maximum of justice, to deplore deviations from justice and to denounce abuses and excesses and social evils'. To suggest technical ways of bringing about justice, however, is beyond its task as the question is limited, historical and changes according to time, place and situation'. The booklet also further clarified its difference from the ICP as primarily one of world-views. That of the ICP, they stressed, had serious consequences: 'Once a party has categorized religion as an enemy, it causes a corresponding negative attitude in anyone who does not want to renounce his religion'. Here, they pointed out, was the value of their movement. While adopting the actual policies of the ICP, it simultaneously freed them of their ideological superstructures.

There were two positive results: 'First, the Catholic worker no longer finds any reason to reject these policies; second, the non-Catholic worker loses every reason to maintain his ideological rigidity . . .' Moreover, if a mass of Catholics 'fight for a Communist idea, it bears witness to the fact that the dialectical materialistic ideology is not indispensable . . . for the political energy of the proletariat' and that 'religion . . . is not a bourgeois ideology, a brake on political action'.[7]

AFTER WORLD WAR II

Immediately after the war, Franco Rodano, one of the young intellectuals of the movement (today a practising Catholic and member of the ICP), further illustrated their thesis on the superiority of historical to dialectical materialism. In his article published in their newspaper *Voce Operaia* (17 July 1944) he showed that historical materialism had nothing to do with economic determinism. He referred to the works of Marx, Lenin and Gramsci, which underline their opposition to any form of fatalism and the 'importance of action as the necessary and final catalyst of mechanistic contrasts within the productive forces'; 'the intervention of the free energy of man is necessary to change the face of the earth'. After other examples, Rodano concluded that the 'history of Marxism is the history of its progressive liberation from the most materialistic of all concepts that of ''fatalism'' which in turn is the very foundation of every materialistic philosophy'. Thus historical materialism was an acceptable path to follow as 'it is the duty of Catholics, and of all who have the interest of the human person at heart, to struggle against every fatalistic and deterministic concept and deformation, for these always deny the essence of the person by destroying his liberty'.[8]

'After the war, the Vatican had not yet decided that the ''political unity of Catholics'' would be its official position. Thus, there were high-level, tense discussions about the possible value of many Catholic parties—conservative, moderate and left-wing. Ottaviani, Tardini and Ghedda held this last position, Montini was for 'the political unity of Catholics'.[9] In September 1944, the CCM together with other left-wing Catholic groups, formed the short-lived Christian Left Party, disbanded by its leaders in December 1945.

The majority experienced their 'diaspora' as militant, well-prepared, left-wing Catholics among Italy's secular left.[10] Nor were they asked to be less. The esteem they had acquired during the armed resistance had its immediate effects. A few days after disbanding, the ICP at its fifth congress modified its statutes and accepted members of any religious or philosophical conviction, provided they accepted the policies and programmes of the party. The patient work of these left-wing Catholics was one of the principal factors behind the Socialists' but especially the ICP's position with respect to men of faith and religion, without which the present move to the left of so many (qualified) Catholic laymen and priests is inexplicable.

From an inter-church viewpoint, their forty-years witness to, and theoretical elaboration of, a 'believer-historical Marxist' position, their avoidance of any form of syncretism, and their defence of religion, of the Church and of the validity of the Gospel for all generations and in all cultures explains one of the bases for the strong and ever-growing[11] conviction in Italy that one can be left-wing and a 'good Catholic'. These factors could be, and from a pastoral point of view perhaps should be, the sufficient ground upon which to reconsider open dialogue with the left-wing Catholics and their eventual acceptance as first-class citizens in the Italian Catholic Church.

Notes

1. *Bollettino della Doxa* (Milan, 1973) Year XXVII, No. 14, p. 214 (the Doxa Institute is a member of the International Association of Public Opinion Institutes).

2. M. Coccni & P. Montesi, *Per una storia della sinistra cristiana* (Rome, 1975), pp. 10-13.

3. Ibid., 'I nostri doveri,' p. 14.

4. The word 'Sinarchico' means 'Contrary to anarchic' or 'without anarchy'; 'Unifying' was the closest single word, but lacks the historical significance.

5. Carlo F. Casula, 'Lo scioglimento della sinistra cristiana', in *I cattolici tra fascismo e democrazia* (Bologna, 1975), pp. 302-5.

6. Cocchi, op. cit., 'Il manifesto del Partito cooperativista sinarchico,' pp. 15, 43-47, 55-57.

7. Ibid., 'Il comunismo e i cattolici', pp. 100-101, 109, 116-17.

8. Franco Rodano, 'Il materialismo storico e la libertà dell'uomo' in *Voce Operaia* (July 17, 1944).

9. Franco Rodano, from an interview of April 6, 1977 with this author in which permission was given to quote this fact.

10. S. Lombardini, 'Alcune Riflessioni sulle esperienze della Sinistra Cristiana', in *Cen. Doc. Cath. Dem. Quarderni* (Rome, 1977) I, pp. 38-46.

11. *Bollettino della Doxa*, year XVII (1963) nos. 4-5, p. 35; year XXVIII (1974) no. 14, pp. 111-15.

PART IV

Theory

Rudolf Siebert

Communication Without Domination

SINCE the mid-nineteen sixties, ideology criticism has been the *leit-motif* of much western sociology, philosophy and theology, among dialecticians and positivists alike. Ideology is understood in the critical sense as justification of unjustifiable relations of domination. Ideology is apology for indefensible contradictions in advanced industrial society, between the individual and the collective, luxury and misery, the producer and the consumer, and rich and poor classes. It is an appearance necessary to stabilize an antagonistic advanced and post-capitalist society. It is false consciousness of a false world split into rich and poor nations and hemispheres. One of the most outstanding critics of ideology in Europe and America is the social philosopher Jürgen Habermas.

COMMUNICATIVE ACTION

In the context of the Frankfurt School's critical theory of society, the Hegelian Habermas established his own unique positive by developing a critical theory of communicative action.[1] In his theory Habermas sees the subjectivity of man, just as his intersubjectivity which precedes it, primarily as a potential for foundations admitting of truth. For Habermas, the subjectivity of man consists in the possibility of specifying rational grounds in intersubjective communication, or of man being able to accommodate himself to such grounds or to the refutation of his own grounds. Habermas intends in his critical philosophy of communicative practice to salvage the principle of free subjectivity and intersubjectivity, which is of Christian origin and originally grounded in transcendence, and in a humanistic form through advanced and post-capitalist into post-modern society. While Habermas reflects in his

81

dialectical sociology of communicative action upon the actual communication process in capitalist and socialist society, as it is systematically distorted by ideology rooted in structures of domination of man
by man, he anticipates at the same time an ideal speech situation or
communication without force in post-modern reconciled society.

At present the Christian faith is challenged by ideologies everywhere
and ideologies exist in the Church itself.[2] Ideologies distort communication between the Church and advanced industrial society as well as
among individuals and groups in the Church. Habermas's hermeneutical-dialectical philosophy of communication can help theologians
to de-ideologize and precisely thereby to improve communication between the Church and organized capitalist and post-capitalist society as
well as in the Church: between laity and clergy, the communicators and
communicants of the Christian message, the theologians and the
bishops, the pope and married and divorced people, the hierarchy and
the Catholic Left, the bishops and the estranged priests, the bishops
and the Catholic press. Habermas's hermeneutical-dialectical approach to subjectivity and intersubjective communication can serve as
a basic theory for the development of a theology of communicative
practice undistorted by ideology: a dialectical ecclesiology of communication without domination.[3]

LANGUAGE, LABOR AND INTERACTION

According to Habermas's basic book *Knowledge and Human Interests,* all empirical-scientific, philosophical and theological knowledge is
determined by individual and collective interests, particularly class
interests.[4] The cognitive interests which guide and motivate all knowledge find their place in Habermas's critical theory of communication in
a tripartite scheme.[5] The three dimensions of the scheme are spheres of
dialectical mediation which socialize and humanize men and women
who enter into them. The three mediating areas form the fundamental
topography of Habermas's theory. This topography has its philosophical roots in Hegel's dialectical social philosophy.

Against the trend of modern philosophy from Descartes to Kant to
concern itself merely with the solitary reflection of a single self-
consciousness in finished form, Hegel from his *Early Theological Writings* on sets himself the task to unfold the process of man's becoming
human in the context of self-consciousness and *ipso facto* of freedom
as man's being at home with himself in communication with others, as
his identity with himself in solidarity with others.[6]

According to Hegel's *Jenaer System Drafts,* the culminating dimension among the three mediating spheres of language, tool, and recogni-

tion is the last: the area of dominion, mastery or governance, of lord-ship. The dimension of lordship in Hegel's system drafts bears a manifest relation to that most influential of his themes, entitled 'Lord and Bondsman', in his *Phenomenology of Spirit* of 1806.[7] In Hegel's perspective, the milieu of dominion is the domain of intersubjective communication, in which the struggle for human recognition leads to the unstable hierarchy of master and servant. It ultimately comes to its resolution only in a society of reciprocal recognition among equals, who recognize themselves as mutually recognizing one another. In Hegel's view, a fully human self-consciousness is achieved only through the recognition of the consciousness and the freedom of the other, as for instance in the dialectic of love between husband and wife. It is Hegel's realization that no one man or woman can be free as long as not all men and women are free, that motivates the high humanistic aspirations of the dialectical sociologists of the Frankfurt School. The categorical imperative of the Frankfurt School is 'Act as if the interest in the solidarity with humanity and the emancipation of humanity were your own existential interest'.[8]

Like Hegel and unlike Marx, Habermas differentiates sharply between the sphere of labour and the dimension of interaction aiming at solidarity and at a meaningful emancipation, the happiness of communicative experience, and puts more emphasis on the latter than on the former. Habermas applies the Frankfurt School's imperative rooted in the sphere of interaction, not only to family, society, state, history, art, philosophy and science, but to religion.

BEYOND IDEOLOGY

According to Habermas, using words of Friedrich Schelling that reach back into Western mysticism, the distorted world and a humanity that is concealed from itself manifest their curse in the domination of the external over the internal, of the lower over the higher, of anger over love, of the force of the dark sentiments over purity and clarity.[9] Habermas argues that on this same experience of the contradictory character of the world is based the prejudgment of Marx's historical materialism, which grants priority of the economic basis of capitalist society over its cultural superstructure. Habermas, like Marx, does not accept the barbaric power with which the economic conditions in liberal, organized and post-capitalist society hold determinate sway over all that is more sublime—art, religion, philosophy, science—as a sign of the ontological structure of the world, which must remain as it is for ever. Instead Habermas considers this power of the material basis in capitalist and in socialist society to be the sign of the governance of nature over society. For Habermas this governance is historical and can therefore be overthrown in the course of history as man's self-enlightening, self-emancipating and self-formative process of becoming. As long as this has not yet happened, the natural condition subjects the system of social life to the yoke of the process of reproduction in its naked economic form.

In Habermas's view, because Ernst Bloch, in returning to Marx's theory of religion as contained in the latter's theses on Feuerbach, explicitly re-establishes the practical significance of ideology criticism, he can go beyond the critique of religious ideology summarized in the Marxian theses.[10] Marx states in the fourth thesis, that Feuerbach proceeds from the fact of man's religious self-alienation, the duplication of the world into a religious and a secular one. In Marx's view, Feuerbach's accomplishment consists in resolving the religious superstructure back into its secular basis. But in Marx's perspective, that this earthly basis elevates itself above itself and establishes itself as an independent realm above the daily practical life-world of people, can be explained only as the result of the internal ruptures and self-contradiction in this secular basis. According to Marx, the worldly basis of civil society must thus be understood both in its dialectical contradictions and convulsions and revolutionized in practice.

But the religious world above, so Habermas argues with Bloch, is so intimately a part of its earthly basis, the need, production and exchange systems of capitalist society, that the idea of God is debased, distorted and made use of as ideology by the inner antagonisms that sunder the capitalist world, yet without wholly being dissolved into this ideology. Habermas has no doubt that the world of religion emerges as a product of the dialectical contradictions in the secular world of oligopolistic late capitalist society, yet at the same time transcends it. If all this is correct, Habermas agrees with Bloch, then the false consciousness of a false world is not simply nothing. For as the negation of the negation—the antagonistic capitalist society—though not consciously as such, religion is still full of encoded human experience. Within the ideological shell of religion, Habermas like Bloch, Horkheimer, Adorno, Marcuse and Fromm, discovers the concrete and real utopian core, within the false ideological consciousness the true consciousness. According to Habermas, the transparency of a better world, as represented mythically or theologically by religion, is refracted by hidden interests, often class interests, even in those aspects, which, being utopian and as such subversive, point beyond the organized and post-capitalist society. But still the hopes which the transparency of a reconciled world in religion awakens in people, the longings which it justifies, contain energies that at the same time, once instructed about themselves by the critical theory of communicative practice, turn into critical if not revolutionary impulses.

IDENTITY

According to Habermas, following Hegel's philosophy of religion, it is only the major universal religions, of which Judaism and Christianity are the most rationally structured, which raise a universalistic truth claim.[11] The one, other-worldly, providential and wholly just, gracious, and loving God of Christianity leads to the formation of an ego-identity in the believer, severed from all concrete rôles and norms of his particular society or state. This 'I' of the believer can know itself as a completely singular being in God's universal love. The idea of the immortal soul in the face of the loving God opens up the path to the idea, that, as Hegel puts it, the individual has infinite worth and is determined to the highest, most liberated subjectivity.[12] Here in Christianity, so Habermas argues, the carrier of the religious system is no longer the family, tribe, or the city state, as in earlier primitive mythical or polytheistic religions, but the community of believers, to which potentially all men and women belong, since the commands of the one God are universal. To be sure, the highly developed traditional, liberal, or modern capitalist civilizations are all class societies with extreme inequalities in the distribution of power and wealth. On the one hand, therefore, the political system of those civilizations need legitimation to a high degree. On the other hand, the potential of monotheistic religions to provide universalistic justification is not designed to satisfy the particularistic demand of the political system of the highly evolved civilizations. In Habermas's view, at this state of social evolution the religious meaning systems and the political imperatives of self-maintenance in these highly differentiated civilizations become incompatible. Hence a counterfactual *nexus* must be formed between the legitimizing potential of the universal religions, particularly Christianity, and the existing political order, whether in traditional, liberal or organized capitalist societies. This is the function of ideology. According to Habermas, ideology functions as the counterweight to the structural similarities between a particular collective identity tied to the particular state and self-identities of individuals formed within the framework of the universalistic religious associations. In Habermas's view, this problem of identity inheres in all the developed civilizations. But it becomes fully conscious only in the modern age, with the arrival of the liberal capitalist state, because until then a series of mediating mechanisms had been operative: earlier identity formations remain widespread in traditional society, as indicated by symbols and rituals of a pagan origin, for instance, magic and mythical elements in medieval Catholicism; the distinction between the members of the community of believers and its addressees outside still held in the sway of pagan beliefs; the dualism of divine transcendence and an almost entirely secular world in terms of a dualistic theism.

COMMUNICATION STRUCTURE

In Habermas's as in Hegel's view, with the modern era these and other mediating mechanisms have evidently become ineffective.[13] With Protestantism many of the pre-Christian elements, assimilated by medieval Catholicism, were discarded. This in turn reinforced the demand for strictly universalist commitments and the corresponding individualistic structure of the individual's self. As the Catholic Church split up at the end of the Middle Ages into a multiplicity of churches, denominations and sects, the membership of the individual in a community of believers lost not only its exclusiveness, but its rigid institutional ties.

In Habermas's perspective, in the second half of the twentieth century there has been a significant shift in the direction of theological currents, giving a radical this-worldly interpretation to the Christian message of salvation and tending to obliterate completely the traditional dualistic theism. According to Habermas, the repoliticization of the biblical inheritance in contemporary theological discussion, particularly in the critical political theology of W. Pannenberg, Jürgen Moltmann, Dorothee Sölle, Johannes B. Metz, Gustavo Gutierrez and Rubem Alves, who are strongly committed to ideology criticism, goes with a levelling off of the this-worldly/other-worldly dichotomy and points to the destruction of traditional dualistic theism. Habermas does admit that the repoliticization of the Christian gospel of redemption, carried on in critical theology, does not mean outright atheism in the sense of a liquidation without any trace of the idea of God. But Habermas seriously doubts that the idea of a personal God can be salvaged with consistency from the critical thought produced by the political theology. In Habermas's view, in critical theology the idea of God is transformed into the concept of a *logos* that determines the community of the believers and the real-life world of a self-enlightening and self-emancipating society. God, Habermas argues, becomes for the political theologians the sign of little more than a communicative structure that forces men, on pain of a loss of their humanity, to go beyond their accidental, empirical subjectivity to encounter one another indirectly: that is, across an objective something that they themselves are not, a wholly Other.

According to Habermas, de-ideologized political theology characterizes a development in advanced capitalist society in which what is
left of universal religions, especially Christianity, is merely the core of
universal moral systems; and this is the more so, the more transparent
the infrastructure of monotheistic belief-systems—the capitalist production and exchange process—has become. In Habermas's view,
Hegel perceived the initial phase of this development of radical secularization as well as its tremendous practical consequences: the inevitable cleavage between the self-identity of the single person derived
from the universalistic meaning structure of Christianity and the collective identity bound up with a particular nation—or super nation state.

Following Hegel's suggestion to go beyond a traditional dualistic
toward a modern dialectical theism, enabling men and women living in
advanced industrial society to see the Infinite in the finite and the finite
in the Infinite in terms of a united world-view without losing the idea of
a personal God, and precisely thereby to reconcile in themselves their
personal and collective identity, Habermas decided to move toward
atheistic humanism.[14] This is the limit of Habermas's philosophy. In
order to arrive at a critical theology of communicative practice, we
must go beyond Habermas. We can do this only by recourse to Hegel's
dialectical philosophy of right and religion.

CONSCIENCE

For Hegel, the true social morality is God's universal Spirit living in
the human self-consciousness as it exists in its real presence as a particular nation and as individuals. The individual's self-consciousness as
it reflects back into itself from its external empirical reality, and as it
lifts its universal truth fully into its consciousness, has in its faith and
conscience only what it possesses in the certitude of itself, in its
spiritual reality. In Hegel's view, the empirical and the spiritual reality
of man's self-consciousness is inseparable. In Hegel's perspective, two
different types of conscience cannot exist: a religious and a socio-
ethical conscience, the second of which would differ in content from
the former when directing communicative action in family, society,
state, history or Church. But in terms of form—that is, for thought—
the religious content of conscience as the pure truth in and for itself and
therefore the highest, absolute, and universal truth, has the function of
legitimizing social morality, which is in empirical reality and guides
communicative practice.

According to Hegel, it is the monstrous error of modern times to
consider the inseparability of religious and socio-ethical conscience to
be separable and to see the two consciences as indifferent toward each

other. Philosophers of the bourgeois Enlightenment saw the relationship of universal religion to the particular state so that the latter with all its communicative interaction already existed for itself without any grounding by the universal religion, out of some kind of secular power of authority. For those philosophers, religion was merely a private subjective concern of individuals. To add it as a stabilizing factor to a state already equilibrated in-and-for-itself could be desirable or a matter of indifference.

DUALISTIC THEISM

In the face of the material inseparability of religious and socio-ethical conscience, it is of interest to Hegel to show the actual separation between them in the aspect of religion.[15] This separation concerns first of all the form: that is, the relationship of the believer's self-consciousness to the content of universal religious truth. Since this content is the substance of God's universal Spirit's presence in the believer's self-consciousness in its empirical reality, it finds self-certainty in this content, and is liberated in it. But, in Hegel's view, it is nevertheless possible for the relationship of unfreedom to occur in religion in terms of form, in spite of the fact that its content in-and-for-itself is God's universal Spirit. Hegel finds this great difference of content and form within the Christian religion of truth and freedom itself.

It was Hegel's view that the Catholic Church of his time was determined by a notionless dualistic theism, with major consequences for communicative practice in the church. In the Catholic religion, so Hegel argues, God's universal spirit is in reality rigidly in opposition to the believer's self-conscious spirit. Dualistic theism limits not only man's self-consciousness and self-determination, but God's infinite Spirit, and whereas it asserts the latter's infinity, it nevertheless denies it unconsciously at the same time. It makes implausible the Christian belief in God's first creation, his incarnation in the man Jesus, and the second genesis of a new heaven and earth. Dualistic theism holds to the Greek *chorismos* between the Infinite and the finite and systematically distorts communicative practice in the Church. How?

In Hegel's perspective, dualistic theism, a tradition broken only by a few dialectical theologians for instance, Master Eckhart and Nicholas of Cusa, first distorts the communicative practice of the eucharist. According to Hegel, in the Catholic Church of his time God is represented to the devotion of the believers in the wafer as an external, quasi-natural thing. While Hegel accepts the objectivity of God's presence in the sacrament of the altar, he is nevertheless critical of the element of externalization and reification in the Catholic practice of the eucharist. Therefore Hegel has a certain preference for the Lutheran teaching on the eucharist, since in the Lutheran Church the host is consecrated and elevated into the objective presence of God in. the believer's act of reception: that is, in the destruction of the objectivistic externality of the wafer; and in faith: that is, in the simultaneously free self-conscious spirit of the believer.

In Hegel's view, from the first and highest relationship of reification, dualistic theism, there flow other external, thereby unfree, unspiritual and even superstitious relationships (which he observed in Catholic churches in Berlin and elsewhere in Germany and Europe in the first decades of the nineteenth century). Hegel is critical of the fact that the laity as a status group receives the knowledge of divine truth as well as the direction of will and conscience entirely from outside: that is, from another status group, the clergy. The relationship between clergy and laity has similarities to that between lord and bondsman in antiquity or the Middle Ages. Even the clergy does not possess the knowledge of the truth in a spiritual way alone, but needs an external and reified consecration to do so. Furthermore, Hegel opposes the merely lip-moving, unspiritual mode of prayer; the fact that the believer relinquishes immediate direction to God and asks others for intercession; devotion to miraculous pictures, even to saints' bones, and the expectation of miracles through them; in general, justification through external works; merit which is supposed to be acquired through works and can even be transferred to others; and so on. According to Hegel, these often opaque and fossilized traditions keep the believer's spirit captive in externality and thereby alienated. Through such captivity, the very notion of man's self-consciousness is mistaken and perverted; right and justice, social morality and conscience, accountability and duty are essentially corrupted and communicative action is distorted not only in the Church but in the state.

In Hegel's view, dualistic theism and the consequent development of unfreedom in the Christian community are paralleled by a legislation and a constitution of bondage in the secular realm of abstract right and a condition of injustice and immorality in the sphere of family, society, state, and history. Hegel was aware that the Catholic religion in his time had been praised very loudly by conservative and reactionary statesmen, à la Metternich, as the religion which alone secured the stability of governments. In Hegel's view, an externalized and therefore unfree religion can indeed become a factor of equilibration, but only for governments which are connected with institutions founded on the unfreedom of man's spirit (which ought to be free in terms of private right and social morality): that is, on institutions of injustice and on conditions of socio-ethical corruption and barbarism. From South American Catholic states Hegel draws the conclusion, that among Catholics the spiritual foundation of mutual confidence cannot take place, since in the secular affairs of Catholic states only force and voluntary submissiveness prevail and the political forms, which here are called constitutions are merely an expedient.[16] Much has changed in Catholicism since Hegel's time, particularly since Leo XIII's social encyclical letter *Rerum Novarum*. But much more has still to be changed.

RECONCILIATION THROUGH DIALECTICS

Towards the end of his philosophy of religion, Hegel states that insofar as in the process of enlightenment thinking begins reflectively to oppose the actual world of life, particularly religious traditions, it is internally necessary for thought to work through this opposition between religious and secular consciousness until it arrives at reconciliation.[17] This reconciliation is the philosophy of religion. Insofar as this philosophy is reconciliation, it is dialectical theology. This theology represents the reconciliation of God with himself and with nature. That nature, as God's other, is nevertheless divine in itself, and man's finite spirit is partially in itself this: to elevate itself to reconciliation with God and with itself and partially to come to such reconciliation in world history, in state, society, family, and marriage.

In Hegel's view, this religious knowledge through the dialectical notion, this dialectical theology of reconciliation, is by its very nature not empirically universal. It is merely knowledge in the Christian community. During the bourgeois Enlightenment, three different groups are formed in this community of believers. The first group consists of believers who were still committed to an immediate naive religion and mythical faith. The second group was on the level of analytical understanding. They were the 'educated' believers. They participated in and were deeply affected by reflection, enlightenment, and emancipation. The third group of believers consisted of dialectical theologians.

At the end, his philosophy of religion depicts the Christian Church in modern times as falling into the disunion of naive and educated believers. It seems to him that the Church's completion is at the same time its destruction. But Hegel the dialectical theologican refuses to speak of the destruction of the Christian community since, according to the New Testament, the kingdom of God is founded for eternity.

But Hegel is seriously dedicated to truth and knows that it does not make sense to deny this dissonance, since it is inherent in the empirical reality of modern society itself. Hegel finds that in antagonistic civil society private moral opinion and conviction without objective truth have made themselves uniquely valid. In bourgeois society, the passion for private right, particularly the acquisition of property, and the mania of pleasure are the order of the day. For the immediate consciousness of the bourgeois no unity any longer exists between internality and externality, and nothing is any longer justified in faith. The severity of an objective command, or external discipline, or the power of the state or the Church can no longer be effective. For such controls, the ruin of communicative interaction has gone too deep. When the gospel is no longer preached to the poor, when the salt has lost its savour, and when all religious foundations have quietly been removed by the analytical understanding of enlightenment, then the simple people for whose stunted reason the truth can only appear in a naive mythical representation are powerless when they sense the urge of their spirit for religion as consciousness of the absolute truth. The simple people are still closest to the infinite pain of love as the power uniting that which is torn asunder. But since the enlighteners have perverted love into love and pleasure without pain, the people have been abandoned by their teachers.

In his philosophy of religion as dialectical theology, Hegel dissolves the dissonances, the contradictions in the communicative interaction in Church and society by reconciling subjective opinion and conviction and objective truth and validity, internality and externality, faith and reason, individual and Church and state, gospel and enlightenment, notion and myth, love and pain, finitude and infinitude, accidental and substantial subjectivity, salvation and emancipation. Hegel discovers in the Christian message the absolute truth and God's universal spirit. But as Hegel is aware of the fact that the dialectical theology of reconciliation is only a particular one and as such without external universality, he comprehends it as a sanctuary set apart from antagonistic civil society. The dialectical theologians form an isolated priesthood. They are not allowed to conform to contradictory bourgeois society. They must salvage and guard the possession of the absolute truth—the communicative trinitarian idea of God—through the present world-historical transition period, which Hegel announced already in his *Phenomenology,* towards a new post-modern society in which the social contradictions of civil society will be dissolved and faith, reason, individual and community will be in balance.[18]

COMMUNICATION COMMUNITY

At this point, Habermas criticizes Hegel, with some justification. He says that the Heraclitean philosopher has never completely departed from the soil of the basic Parmenidean prejudice, which has lived on in western philosophy and theology: that the many are excluded from participation in being.[19] According to Habermas, the continence of Hegel's dialectical theology of reconciliation in relation to immediate communicative practice in contemporary society and Church mirrors its superiority and, at the same time, its impotence in the face of danger so full of practical consequences: that is, the demoralization of people living in advanced and post-capitalist society as a result of de-mythologization. With the help of Habermas's theory of communicative action, Hegel's dialectical theology can be universalized and put into practice, which is not foreign to his philosophy in general.[20]

Through Habermas's theory of communicative practice, Hegel's dialectical theology of reconciliation can be transformed into a universal and practical theology of communicative action. While the method of such a theology would be hermeneutical-dialectical, its task would be, negatively, to overcome dualistic theism and the externalized and reified traditions connected with it and, positively, to rediscover dialectical theism and to transform the Church in its light into a community of critical communication.[21] In the universal Church as a communicative community, believers participate in practical discourse. In such discourse believers test the claim to validity of traditional and newly-developed norms of faith and personal and social morality. To the extent that believers accept these norms with reasons, they arrive at the conviction that in the given circumstances of advanced, post-capitalist or post-modern society the proposed norms are right. The truth claim of norms is no longer grounded in the irrational volitional acts of groups of naïve or enlightened believers in opaque, fossilized traditions, or in irrational authorities, but in the rationally motivated recognition of norms by believers. Such recognition of norms may be questioned by believers at any time, as the circumstances arising in advanced industrial or post-modern society demand. The cognitive component of the norms is not limited to the propositional content of normative behavioural expectations. The normative validity claim is in itself cognitive in the sense of the supposition, however contrary to fact, that it could be discursively redeemed by believers, that it is grounded in the consensus of the believers participating in discourse through argumentation in the universal Church as a communicative community.

With the support of a universalized and practical theology of communication, believers can thematize in the Church as communicative community the routines of the normative contents and values embodied by specific norms of faith and morality, and can thereby render them accessible to communicative practice. Believers confused by the present transition period and its transvaluation of all values and norms, can find new personal and social identities in the consciousness of a universal and equal opportunity to participate in value and norm-forming learning processes in the Church as a communicative community. Theological legitimacy presupposes value and normative communication. In the Church as a communicative community, the communicative structure of universal practical discourse obtains because, in the present historical transition, the formation of tradition has been forced out of its natural and unconscious conditions, and because therefore the basic consensus of the believers on belief and value systems can now be reached only through the medium of general discourse. In the face of more or less understood, comprehended, or even doubted traditions, believers have to choose between further disintegration of the Christian community on the one hand or grass-roots communication on the other. *The layman, priest, bishop, pope who avoids general discourse invites disaster.*[22]

The limits of ecclesiastical administrative interference with tradition and the compulsion to communicate mobilization of tradition in the present Church, reveal that very structure around which alone new personal and social identities can crystallize towards the future Church as a communicative community. They would be identities, non-prejudiced in their content, and independent of particular organizational types. They would be identities of believers who engage in the discourse and experimental formation of an indentity-related religious knowledge on the basis of a critical appropriation of tradition as well as of inputs from the positive natural and social sciences, the arts and philosophy. The temporal structure of a future-oriented remembrance in the communicative Church would allow believers to develop universalistic ego-structures on the basis of individual identities (cf. Karl Rahner's Christian of the future).[23] Any position in the Church can agree with any other position in its support for a future universality: in solidarity with humanity on the way to the emancipation of mankind, and beyond that to God's kingdom.

Notes

1. J. Habermas, *Legitimation Crisis* (Boston 1975), pp. 130-43; J. Habermas, *Kultur und Kritik* (Frankfurt am Main, 1973), pp. 195-231.

2. L. Zimmerer, 'Christlicher Glaube und Ideologie', in *Frankfurter Hefte* (FH) 20, 9 (July 1963), pp. 447-54; L. Teinisch, 'Christen in der kommunistischen Welt', *FH* 19, 8 (August, 1964), pp. 527-30; R. Bohne, 'Die Entdeckung der Gerechtigkeit', *FH* 29, 9 (September, 1974), pp. 647-55; W. Dirks, 'Ghetto im Angriff', *FH* 17, 5 (May, 1962), pp. 295-98; W. Dirks, 'Bittere Frucht', *FH* 19, 8 (August, 1964), pp. 533-40; E. Höflich, 'Ideologien in der Kirche', *FH* 20, 9 (September, 1965), pp. 637-46.

3. H. Peukert, *Wissenschaftstheorie-Handlungstheorie-Fundamentale Theologie* (Düsseldorf, 1976), III, D.

4. J. Habermas, *Knowledge and Human Interests* (Boston, 1971), part I, pp. 301-17.

5. J. Habermas, 'Knowledge and Interest', *Inquiry*, IX (1966), pp. 291-95; J. Habermas, *Theory and Practice* (Boston, 1971) ch. 4; J. Habermas, *Kultur*, p. 202.

6. G. W. F. Hegel, *On Christianity: Early Theological Writings* (New York, 1948), pp. 302-8, 309-19.

7. G. W. F. Hegel, *Phänemenologie des Geistes* (Stuttgart, 1964), pp. 148-58.

8. G. Radnitzky, *Contemporary Schools of Metascience* (New York, 1970), II, pp. 164, 170.

9. Habermas, *Theory*, pp. 235-36.

10. *Ibid.*, p. 239; K. Marx, *Die Fruhschriften* (Stuttgart, 1953), pp. 339-41; M. Horkheimer, *Die Sehnsucht nach dem ganz Anderen* (Hamburg, 1971), pp. 60-62.

11. J. Habermas, 'On Social Identity', *Telos* 19 (Spring, 1974), pp. 92-93.

12. *Ibid.*; G. W. F. Hegel, *Enzyklopädie* (Hamburg, 1959), p. 388; G. W. F. Hegel, *Grundlinien der Philosophie des Rechtes* (Stuttgart, 1964), pp. 182-83, 265-67; G. W. F. Hegel, *Vorlesungen über die Philosophie der Religion* (Stuttgart, 1965), I, p. 35.

13. Habermas, 'On Social Identity', pp. 93-94; Habermas, *Legitimation Crisis*, p. 121.

14. Habermas, 'On Social Identity', pp. 84-103; Hegel, *Vorlesungen I*, p. 34; H. Küng, *Menschwerdung Gottes* (Freiburg, 1970), p. 558; H. Küng, *Christ sein* (Munich, 1974), pp. 285, 299, 348, 367.

15. Hegel, *Enzyklopädie*, p. 433.

16. *Ibid.*, p. 433; G. W. F. Hegel, *Vorlesungen über die Philosophie der Geschichte* (Stuttgart, 1961), pp. 126-7.

17. Hegel, *Vorlesungen II*, pp. 354-56.

18. *Ibid.*, 223-47, 247-308, 308-56, 355-56; Hegel, *Phänomenologie*, pp. 18-20; Hegel, *Grundlinien*, p. 320; G. W. F. Hegel, *Asthetik* (Frankfurt-am-Main, 1952), II, p. 423.

19. Habermas, *Theory*, pp. 189-91.

20. M. Theunissen, *Hegel's Lehre vom absoluten Geist als theologisch-politischer Traktat* (Berlin, 1970), pp. 3-26, 387-419; Hegel, *Vorlesungen*, pp. 43-47.

21. Habermas, *Legitimation Crisis*, pp. 105, 110; Habermas, 'On Social Identity', 101-3.

22. W. Dirks, 'Volkskirche im Übergang-Zur Krise der Kirche', I, *FH* 25 (February, 1970), pp. 108-16; II, 25, 3 (March, 1970), pp. 187-93; W. Dirks, 'Der Papst gegen die Kirche', *FH* 23, 9 (September, 1968), pp. 621-29; W. Dirks, 'Der Papst, der Friede und die Eheleute', *FH* 21, 12 (December, 1966), pp. 835-42; W. Dirks, 'Die sogenannte Verwirrung der Gläubigen', *FH* 20, 8 (August, 1965), pp. 533-38; W. Dirks, 'Kann die Kirche demokratisch werden'? *FH* 24, 7 (July, 1969), pp. 469-76; I. Hermann, 'Die Romisch-Katholische Kirche und ihre Konflikte', *FH* 28, 8 (August 1973), pp. 565-72.

23. K. Rahner, *The Christian of the Future* (New York & London, 1968), pp. 77-101.

Wolfgang Bartholomäus

Communication in the Church: Aspects of a Theological Theme

COMMUNICATION AS A THEME IN THEOLOGY

IS 'COMMUNICATION' a theological topic? One is inclined to answer No. If 'communication' refers not only to one ecclesiastical task among others, but to an aspect of the Church itself, then the term and any treatment of it are not to be found in theology.[1] But communication is more than an area of church practice. It refers to a dimension of the existence and activity of the Church itself. There is nothing in the Church which is not open to treatment in terms of a theological communications theory.

The lack is obvious. Whoever takes communications as a theological topic is not primarily concerned with the essence and meaning of the existent itself (texts, traditions, persons, institutions), as in traditional theology. He is interested in the relations and interactions between existents.[2] The existent is examined to see how it relates to others and what effect it takes upon and receives from others. Who or what it may be in itself is a function of this primary interest. 'Theology is not exegetically or systematically concerned with the topic of communication . . . its concern is practical'.[3] It is analytical and prospective. Therefore it does not necessarily include questions concerning the nature of the existent. It extends its area of debate and examination pragmatically. Theology becomes a science which offers explanations of relations and effects in the Church and offers indications towards its improvement, precisely where it is disturbed or disrupted by ideological elements of its own creation.

95

The import of communication as a topic can be estimated from the fact that the Church engages in relations and achieves effects outside the area of intention. Communicative behaviour or action is defined in terms of the communicative effect. But all human behaviour has such an effect. One cannot not communicate. Watzlawick formulates this as a metacommunicative axiom.[4] 'Behaviour or non-behaviour, words or silence all partake of the nature of communication'.[5] To date the Church would seem to have remained blind to this compulsion to permanent communication. The Vatican and the episcopates, priestly dress and the presbytery, the bishop's motor car and the priest's hobby, the way in which theological debates take place in the Church, and the way in which women are treated in the Church: these are all symbolic realities which convey information. They are worthy of examination in terms of a theory of theological communication.

If theology takes up the topic of communication it comes into contact with non-theological sciences. Its primary concern must not then be to use these extra-church disciplines merely to improve its knowledge and thus improve techniques of communication within the Church. Of course any technological deficit ought to be repaired. But a practical theology is primarily concerned with practice, and not with technical questions. It is interested in the meaningful orientation of church practice, and in enabling it to exist at all, not in the mere refinement of technical means. It is therefore confronted with the anthropological implications of the sciences. If communications research takes place in the light of the main question, that is, whether there is a canon of principles in accordance with which it is possible to say what effect a certain communication has on a receiver,[6] then it necessarily reifies the receiver of the communications, insofar as it opines that the subjective human element is causally determined by communications and is not motivated by argument.[7] If, however, it is concerned with finding the conditions for successful understanding by human subjects, who rate their success in understanding one another in terms of a consensus achieved in common,[8] then it is concerned with human beings who are capable of, and ready to attain, subjective agreement in a process of non-dominative communication. In both cases, theology is faced with the question of what its own tradition allows and enables it to do.

Communication can become a theological topic in various ways. In the biblical-Christian tradition, there are motives and impulses for the kind of inter-human relationship which is known as communication. They have to be brought to the level of linguistic discourse and made effective in ecclesiastical action. In this process, hitherto neglected, forgotten or even suppressed, elements of this tradition may be revealed anew. Theology is, of course, more than that. Church communication is disturbed. The reason for that may be that communication can never really succeed in a world of interpersonal and social alienation. But that reason is to be found in the Church itself. The Church features (pseudo-) theological theories and ideologies which hinder communication. Theological theology becomes critical when it undertakes to discover these kinds of behaviour and thought. Since this is still a novel task, more questions than answers attend its progress.

The term 'communication' is not to be restricted in the sense of information theory to the transmission of information between communicators and receptors, nor is it to be understood in the sense of behavioural theory as extensible to any kind of interaction. Communication in the narrow sense exists when partners of equal status *(equality)* exchange *(reciprocity)* communications about their thoughts, feelings and desired actions by means of signs *(symbolic interaction),* and in so doing always communicate something to one another (the aspect of the *content* and *relations* of communication). Communication is not dependent on cause-and-effect relations, nor on stimulus-response links, but on the exchange of communication in signs which are addressed to the reason of the partners and aim at understanding. The partners in the communication process are explicable as a communications system.

In communication with others, the individual extends all forms of existential expression.[9] In communication he achieves the possibilities of cognition (perception, thought), emotion (feelings) and pragmatic-normative behaviour (action, ethics, justice). These forms may be conceived as the result of a mode of existence to which the organism is open and of which the individual is capable as the active and productive subject of its development, the positive realization of which, however, occurs in communication with others. 'In the opportunity of communication utilized by human beings, lies the secret of their spiritual and cultural mode of existence'.[10]

Groups and societies exist through communication. In order to persist, they constantly reassure themselves of the significance of their common thoughts, feelings, and activity. They integrate themselves inwardly and define themselves outwardly. In communication processes they try to correct disturbances which threaten their equilibrium (homeostasis). Because disturbances prevent the system from calcifying and leaving the flux of history, communication is not a resistance against something that ought not to be, but takes on the character of the draft or project, a completion of new possibilities. The equilibrium that ought to be produced is that of an open and dynamic system.

The Christian identity of the individual and of the Church is formed in communication processes. Excommunication is the perversion of those processes. It is only conceivable where individual members of groups do not have enough communicative competence to express themselves comprehensibly and with conviction. Hence they cut off what they no longer find appropriate. The interruption of ecclesiastical discourse by the forms of linguistic complaint and its negation in the 'speechlessness' of repressive ecclesiastical measures always occur when the Church is not adapted to, or mature enough for, the linguistic mode of expression which is expected of it. The guilt correlates positively with the capability of expressing one's intentions.[11] Communication will not succeed if it loses its egalitarian and reciprocal structure.

Between communication in the Church and communication of the Church there is no sharp dividing line. If the 'theologically relevant borders of the Churches and the Church itself are already . . . obscure and certainly very fluid',[12] then its sociological delimitation is also very questionable. The Church has open doors. It is impossible adequately to 'conceive and understand it, if one sees it as a unique entity which is not in principle socially derivable, as in principle opposed to society, as an erratic block in social life, and then isolates it in theological thought or in political argument from its complex interaction with society'.[13] It is just as impossible to remove the individuals concerned in ecclesiastical communication from their social relations. They bring their social being into ecclesiastical communication and into play there. Communication in the Church depends on the fact that the partners show their socially preformed and frequently discrepant expectations and needs. The communicative behaviour of the Church interacts in a multitude of ways with the public communication of society as a whole.

THE CHURCH AS THE SACRAMENT
OF NON-DOMINATIVE COMMUNICATION

Vatican II described the Church as a sacrament. It is an effective symbol of what it characterizes. If the Church is a sign, then it signifies something which it is not itself, and to which it only refers: it signifies the matter of Jesus. It is constitutive of the Church to refer to Jesus and to what has become reality with Jesus. If the Church is also a symbolic sign, then it is in a similar relation to what it designates. Therefore the Church must be an epiphany of the matter of Jesus and refer to the matter of Jesus by means of epiphanic realizations of that concern of Jesus. To refer to a reality which it is not, and at the same time to allow it to become reality within itself, in order to be able to refer to it at all, is the dual requirement placed upon the Church. The tension between not-being and being is essential to the Church.

In the perspective of the theory of theological communications, the matter of Jesus appears as a non-dominative communication made possible by and given by God. Being a Christian is being free. More exactly, being a Christian is being free because, by reason of the unchangeable, finite constitution of men and of imperfect social conditions which can never be completely changed, there will never be any ultimate freedom. Being a Christian is also being free in the sense of progressive or dynamic liberation made possible by God and given by God, and ensured and grasped in encounter with Jesus. Both aspects of this dynamic freedom, its negative and its constructive aspects, freedom from domination [14] and freedom for solidarity, may be conceived as the enablement and capability of non-dominative communication. It is correct to say that this notion of being a Christian, and the idea that it is one's bounden duty, are 'only inconceivable if the Christian is not ready to acknowledge by whom and for what he thinks he is liberated and by whom and for what he wishes to liberate'.[15] Christians have the right to and capability of non-dominative communication, and it is their duty. The Church is the institutionalization and institutional assurance of that freedom.[16]

Jesus himself intended and realized freedom from all suppressive powers and freedom for unlimited communication. He relativized traditional models of thought and behaviour, upset authorities and criticized structures wherever they had become reified as instruments of men's domination of other men. In this way he opened the road to freedom. He did not leave it empty. For the freedom that has been opened up should be realized in unrestricted application to others. Freedom from domination was conceived as freedom for universal solidarity with the exploited and oppressed. This was the freedom that Jesus himself realized in an exemplary fashion. It made possible his unique relationship with God. He was able to be free and to behave freely because in him alienation from God—the ground of all alienation of human beings from one another, as it appears in the reification of man as an object of domination and in the isolation of men from their social needs—was radically cancelled.

The form of non-dominative communication which was given to men and made possible in the sense in which Jesus knew had political dimensions for the early Christians. Acknowledgment of the risen Lord (Rom. 10:9) took concrete form in the early Church as opposition to the domination of the emperor. 'Acknowledgment of the *kyrios* here was opposed to . . . acknowledgment of the *kyrios* there. This confrontation is one of the essential reasons why the Church was treated as an alien body in the State and was officially persecuted by the State'.[17] Christians understood the resurrection and exaltation of Jesus as liberation to their own freedom and claimed this freedom from all new

forms of slavery. Even though Christians nevertheless respected the
dimensions of others' freedom and the inscription of that respect in the
constitution of the State, the reason was that they did not interpret the
freedom of others as a limitation of their own freedom but as an ac-
tualization of their own freedom. They knew that they were made free
for service for the freedom of others. Their own freedom was to be
realized in new communication with others'.[18] They discovered and
experienced the fact that Jesus himself is liberating and liberated existence pure and simple. He is free for God's ultimate presence, free
from any preliminary pressures, free in order to be there radically for
others'.[19]

It is the task of biblical and systematic theology to see whether the
concern of Jesus and the existence of the Church can be conceived
appropriately by means of the category of 'non-dominative communication'.[20] Peukert made an attempt to ground theology as a science on
the basis of communicative behaviour, explicating its normative essence to the point of self-contradiction and absurdity, in the conviction
that the Judaeo-Christian tradition determines the reality of God in
view of the 'paradox of anamnetic solidarity', in which the self-
contradiction and absurdity of communicative behaviour find their extreme realization.[21] Peukert opines that the universal solidarity posited
in communicative behaviour is only taken really seriously if we understand it as solidarity with the generations of the exploited and defeated
before us, which would demand recourse to Judaeo-Christian tradition,
in order to talk of the God who does not 'merely allow those who have
suffered before us to become a datum of past history'.[22] Therefore
non-dominative communicative behaviour is open to theological interpretation.

The relation between ecclesiastical institutions and non-dominative
communication requires explication. The form of institutional-critical
subjectivity raised in the term 'freedom from domination', does not
escape from all forms of union, because in communicative behaviour it
gives rise to relations, and necessarily, therefore, to union. The understanding which communication aims at produces supra-subjective
norms of thought and behaviour which cannot be abolished by individuals of their own volition. They rely on the consensus of all reached
and constantly to be reached through communication, and not on the
formal domination of a few. Moreover, they must assure, not prevent,
consensus and its reproduction. Whoever declares, in view of admitted
disappointments in regard to the possibility of consensus in the
Church, that it is unattainable by non-dominative communication at
present, and that for that reason domination must exist,[23] has to ask
himself what form of anthropology he owes allegiance to. Perhaps he is

an unconscious follower of psychoanalytical anthropology, in which the aboriginal needs of men appear as drives making their demands in spite of the needs of all others, and can only be domesticated by means of repression. He certainly does not follow a theological anthropology which recognizes an aboriginal human socialness, and the fact that the self-communication of God to men has given them new possibilities. But has non-dominative communication in Jesus' sense been radically enough considered and attempted in the Church?

If the Church does not make its essential concerns clear enough, the main reason is not that it contains too many individuals who wickedly exercise power over others and thereby reify men and drive them into isolation. That does happen, of course. Instead one has to start from the far too great readiness of Christians to allow themselves to be dominated. Domination cannot occur against the will of the dominated. It needs agreement. That is all too easily given out of fear and because of the security which people get from it. Non-dominative communication pre-supposes people who in their lives have the possibility of becoming the subjects of their own development. Christian education has often prevented that. The difference between the ideal of non-dominative communication and the reality of dominated isolated men is constitutive of the Church. Because it is a sacrament, the Church is the non-existence and the existence of the matter of Jesus at one and the same time. The ideal appears in the Church but only in a glass darkly. It is only anticipated under the conditions of finite existence and society; it is never fully realized. That is obvious for the Church and no ground for resignation. Yet Christians have to exist and to behave as if non-dominative communication were already here. They have to support it in their communications. Only in that way can they grasp the possibilities of being a Christian. Suffering borne in the tension of non-existence and existence is 'entry into the existential proposal of Jesus',[24] of the one who was crucified for the things he held dear.

THE COURAGE OF SUBJECTIVE COMMUNICATION

Non-dominative communication in Jesus' sense is the yardstick for all communicative behaviour in the Church. The courage of subjective freedom is a condition for ecclesiastical communication. Krappmann has shown the connection between communication and identity.[25] Identity, he says, is both a presupposition and a result of communication. It can be shown how communications problems in the Church are related to identity problems of church communicators. If the individual wants to relate to others, then he has to present himself in his identity, which shows who he is.[26] The individual, however, does not bring his

identity as a pregiven entity into the communications process. He
brings it into communication while taking into account the needs and
expectations of the partner in the process. The partners show their
identities in the needs and expectations which guide them in their present situation. In free subjective interpretation of the identities posited
by the partners, the individual obtains his own identity: an unmistak-
able self-definition of the person as he should enter into the situation,
and with whose needs and expectations he must enter into communication. Those taking part in the process of communication reach—
through reciprocal perception and self-demonstration—understanding
of who they are and how they now wish to behave. Thereby they attain
to and speak to the condition of subjective identity. However paradox-
ical it may sound, this arises from communication processes as a condition of their very possibility.

Every person, including the partner in ecclesiastical communication,
exists simultaneously in different communications systems: in the family, the parish, work, leisure, and so on. These are formal and informal
communications systems which change with time. In them the individual is subjected to divergent requirements. If the individual enters
into new communicative relations with partners, he cannot easily escape the other systems and their demands. If he does not want to
surrender them, he can leave behind neither his present social world
nor his life history to date. If he tries to assert his identity in the new
communication situation, then he is faced not only with the demands of
the new situation but those of other communicative situations. The
previous experiences and the present requirements are the material
from which he is to forge his new identity. Because those experiences
are frequently bound up with unresolved conflicts and problems, the
material resists his moulding work. The ability of the individual to
assert identity in new communications, but at the same time to integrate experiences made elsewhere, even when they are contradictory
and inimical, his ability to assert identity in spite of discrepant requirements is something that Krappmann calls 'equilibrated identity'.[27]
The individual is gifted with activity and creativity in order to assert
identity in this way, and also works with 'a certain amount of uncertainty and the burden of ambivalent self-representation'.[28]

Many church communicators do not possess very much obvious
ability to achieve 'equilibrated identity' in which the individual dem-
onstrates his firmly subjective 'self'. Sometimes it seems as if that kind
of identity was not allowed in the Church. The communicative behaviour of the Church is strongly reminiscent of what Goffmann calls
'total institutionalization'.[29] In total institutions[30] all the interactions of
the members are strictly controlled in form and content. It is not per-

missible for anyone to withdraw any areas of his life from the supervision of the controlling power. The rulers set themselves the express task of ensuring that members of the organization lose their old 'self' and build up a new one. Rôles are comprehensively and unambiguously defined and individuals are required to adopt a completely univocal interpretation of predetermined norms and to surrender their subjectivity under the pressure of major sanctions. Care is taken to ensure that 'individuals orient themselves exclusively to a single notionally relevant rôle'.[31] An attempt is made to ensure that the subjective needs of the members fully concur with the expectations announced from above. Identity and rôle must be one. Whereas elsewhere individuals are allowed to change rôle expectations by means of subjective interpretation, to make the prescribed rôle creatively their own, in this case the essential presupposition is that the individual should totally identify himself with his rôle. The individual must lose himself in the part. The individual becomes a mere player and surrenders any claim to being an active and creative subject.

Paul was able to say that he had become all things to all men: a Jew to the Jews, a man of the law for those who laid down the law, freed from the law to those freed from the law, weak to the weak—for the sake of the Gospel. It was clearly possible for him to redefine himself in each new communicative situation: to say who he was without any fear of losing himself. That does not seem to be permissible for church communicators, even though under the conditions of society as a whole, to which the Church too is subject, equilibrated identity is necessarily expected. Church communicators have to represent the (fixed) belief of the Church, not to formulate their own Christian identities. They have to bring with them what the Church believes and not what they believe. 'In them one encounters only the group, not an individual'.[32] 'One' is more important than 'I'. The category of 'witness' is void under these conditions. Christian testimony requires a man to bring with him his own grasp and experience of belief. Because the Christian and subjective identity of the communicator disappears behind his official front, church communication far too often says nothing at all.

Stable identity, which is fully subject to given rôle expectations and therefore independent of situation and transcendent, can only persist if the communicator stands apart from all relations that might interfere. If the conviction were to spread that church communicators were distant from the lived world of their partners, then they would be in such a condition of self-isolation. The terms 'presbytery', 'clerical dress' and so on indicate regulative modes of behaviour which can be interpreted in terms of theological communications theory as defensive measures undertaken to ward off interference. Self-isolation can also occur in all outside contacts by means of repression or by obfuscating elements of the real world that might cause uncertainty. By such devices, total identification with the communicative rôle is ensured but non-dominative communication is prevented because it requires an ability to demonstrate one's equilibrated identity. It is not surprising that church communicators escape totalitarian demands—for the sake of their very lives and ability to communicate—by living a life 'under the institutional surface'[33] or even giving the whole thing up by seeking laicization.

It is necessary that a desire for individual and subjective experiences should be reborn in the Church. The rulers seem to start from the fiction of total identification with given expectations and not to think it possible that ecclesiastical communicators should have needs which cannot be wholly identified with their rôles. People should not be disqualified in the Church because they ask questions after admitting the disturbing problems of their social environment and their own lives. Non-dominative communication will be possible in the Church when it is openly admitted that heightened subjectivity and individuality produce simultaneous heightening of reciprocal relations between partners.[34]

CRITICAL INTERPRETATION OF REALITY IN FAITH

When theology takes communication as a topic, it treats it crtically. It shows how under the guise of truth ecclesiastical plausibilities and theological presuppositions prevent communication. It examines the existing consensus which supports traditions in regard to the anti-communicative power relations which affect thought, talk and action in the Church.[35] Here theologians have to take into account the fact that the ideological elements of ecclesiastical and theological consciousness have been institutionally reified in the meantime so as to block any critique offered in the interests of future non-dominative communication in the sense Jesus intended.

An initial concern is the content of church communication. Communication has two aspects: content and relation. The content of communications can be grasped in thought and in language. Communications communicate between partners. Partners in communication communicate themselves when they communicate something. They show who they are, what relation there is between them, and in what way the information communicated is to be understood in regard to existing relations. 'The ideal case is when the partners agree about the content of their communications as well as about the definition of their relations'.[36] It is of course necessary that the partners should be basically capable of orderly communication.

The Church is primarily interested in the content of its communications. That shows its unrelenting care for orthodoxy in the sense of conceptual and linguistic accordance with tradition. This is where criticism comes in. We must ask whether discussions which obey only this criterion of truth (by expressing tradition and talking in the language of tradition) are in fact communication. In church communication processes, not only true propositions are admissible. What has to be communicated is the partners themselves. Their expectations and needs have to enter into the communication, and enter into what is said not merely into the way in which it is said. And non-dominative communication dispenses with unilateral subjection. The situation of the partners is the theological source of knowledge for the content and language of church communications. Church communicators may indeed draw truth from their convergence with tradition. The validity of the process stems from convergence with the situation. The theological task undertaken by ecclesiastical communication becomes a critical interpretation of the experienced and experiencable reality of men in faith. The interpretation of tradition is a function of that. Human reality is reflexively conceived in philosophy and the sciences, and insofar as theology stands in a certain relation to them, it works in the same direction. Of course theology has to be more consistently adapted to the process of communication by critical interpretation of reality in faith. Its problem is not 'how on the basis of our experience a new mode of access is to be achieved to a humanly realizable, comprehensible and responsible discourse about God'.[37] Its problem is the appropriate, theologically legitimate way to make the reality of experience itself a symbolic sign of God's liberating presence. Jesus' parables are a model for the theological process here.

In addition, the language of church communication should no longer be controlled from above. The language of church communication makes easier the difficult task of preserving tradition and guarding oneself in the present situation. The traditionalist fixation of church talk by means of doctrinaire and rubricist control of language not only preserves tradition, but acts 'as an instrument of domination, discipline and excommunication'.[38] 'Those who are able to offer the definitions are the lords and masters'.[39] These masters forget how language works. They forget the meanings are brought forth in the very process of communication in common. Anyone who offers definitions before the dialogue begins is certainly the master but in no way a communicator. Fear of masters is growing in the Church. Many church communicators avoid subjective expression, even when they still are capable of it. They enclose themselves linguistically as well. They build bastions against words.

If the critical interpretation of reality in faith is to win some success in church communication both conceptually and linguistically, then the theological interpreters of theory and practice have to put forward their own experience for critical assessment. That will help to cancel the distance of theological tradition and religious experience in a reconcili- ation of doctrine and actual life, which should not remain a private matter but itself become theology.[40] 'Lived theology has to elevate the "subject" to the level of the dogmatic consciousness of theology . . . The subject is the human being who is enmeshed in his experiences and occasions and who constantly identifies himself anew on the basis of them. Introducing the subject into dogmatics also means making the human being in his religious and experiential life the objective theme of dogmatics. It means turning doctrine into life and life into doctrine'.[41] Experiential theology takes the subject's experiences as they are, without forcibly harmonizing them with doctrine, and without sup- pressing conflicts or explaining them away. Communication lives by virtue of dissonance.[42]

FEARLESS RELATIONS AND SPONTANEOUS EMOTIONS

Content can be conveyed only by means of relations. The ability to take up relations has been lost by many church communicators, some- times even systematically purged from them. Church communicators' theological understanding of office by forces them to separate official function and private life. The private aspect which has been fed by life-experiences and conflicts is either repressed (so that, contrary to fact, the conviction can even arise that it was not there at all), or it is schizophrenically split off and nurtured in secret. Both—usually unconscious—mechanisms serve to protect the office from difficulties and questions emanating from the private sphere. But repression and splitting off require energy which could be used for communicative relations. The denial of the private sphere paradoxically interferes with church communications. If one remembers that in the private sphere the real modern world is experienced enrichingly and painfully (the real world which in theology must become the symbol of the freedom of God's activity), then the admission of the private sphere is all the more urgent. Only critical participation in the contemporary world, action in common with one's contemporaries (not on one's contemporaries), participation in their (economic, social, political, cultural) hopes and needs, can restore the ability to undertake communicative relations. Not only personal but structural problems are involved here. So long as priestly celibacy socially isolates the church communicator (at least in western industrial society)—and that appears to be the most important aspect of the sexual side of the problem—no real improvement is to be expected in this field. In addition, in a theological perspective married people (priests, laity, and women) should be admitted to ecclesiastical office, with all the consequences we might expect for thinking, feeling and action in the Church.

Maimed relationships also arise from emotional restrictiveness. The inability of many church communicators to experience and express feelings may be interpreted as a protective measure. Church communicators act in intense emotional situations (birth, marriage, guilt situations, despair situations, sickness, death). They would shatter completely if they were to surrender themselves wholly to them. Probably, the unusual life history those who offer themselves in the service of the Church plays a part here. The same is true of concern with theological science, which conceives the Christian belief which it reflects more as a system of cognitive propositions about God than as emotional relation to God. Of course male society also has an effect on church communicators, who cannot avoid socially-conditioned rôle images of female emotions. Fear of emotions also comes into play, for feelings make one vulnerable, but the Church still avoids sensitivity and its open expression, even though its vulnerability has been notorious for a long time.

Emotional problems have to do with the anthropological body-soul dualism which is not part of authentic Christian tradition but has so strongly affected the past that the present still suffers from it. Fear of physical proximity is a result. The ability to enter into emotional relationships is made possible by the overall personal partnership of mother and child, which is transmitted by the body as the tangibility of the soul.

The interaction of emotions and the body would seem to be confirmed by the observation that the psychosomatically sick are often incapable of experiencing emotions and expressing them.[43] The typical behaviour of psychosomatic patients is often, alas, all too reminiscent of the behaviour of many (especially ordained) church communicators. They do not talk about inner process and feelings but about things. They seem very active but are in fact withdrawn in their relations with other people and are careful not to enter into close and emotionally coloured relationships. They show a unique form of verbal impoverishment. They are hardly able to articulate conflicts and they are extremely reluctant to use emotive words. We might suspect that the fear of physical proximity is the result of a celibate existence which senses the danger of a woman as a potential sexual object and a man as a possible partner for homosexual activity. What Jesus did without any worry when he took children into his arms, touched the ears of the deaf-mute, and laid his hands on the sick, and what he allowed to happen to him when the woman with an issue of blood touched him, and when he allowed Mary Magdalen to anoint him, is something that church communicators have to refind: an undisturbed and fundamental relation to the body and to physical proximity.[44]

Finally, communicative relations are disturbed by the fact that in the Church (by reason of the claims of the *Ecclesia sancta*), fundamentally unattainable ideals of perfection are accepted as normative. Anyone who cannot reach them hides from others and from himself the fact that he is falling behind the ideal norm, but allows his guilt feelings to support his desire to make others fit the ideal. Hence we have a society of total supervision in which everyone (not wanting to be constantly under pressure) subscribes to apparent perfection and tries to impose the same on others by means of rigorous demands. Secretly, people suffer from the experienced difference of ideal from actuality and unburden themselves by the awareness that they are at least suffering from that difference, whereas others obviously are not. Although no one is perfect, everyone appears perfect. But each individual discovers in himself that the opposite is true. The imperfect is repressed in the area of the individual. The social whole continues to practise its appearance of perfection. No one dare admit his imperfection. Whoever reveals the truth counts as an enemy. Tolerance is impossible because one's own guilt feelings do not allow one to become reconciled to oneself and thereby to others. Trust is lacking. And so people separate from one another and become enmeshed in a system of permanent self-deception. Lack of openness, lack of tolerance and almost manic fear of criticism are almost universal (especially among priests). Neurotic reactions are unavoidable. It is often no lasting solution to enter into psychoanalysis and there 'unconditionally to create a repression-free area in which, for the space of the communication between therapist and patient, the real situation, the pressure of social sanctions, is removed as credibly as possible'.[45] The sacrament of penance is inadequate because it cancels the disturbance of communication only in the area of individual guilt. The problem has to be made the object of non-dominative communication in groups. Then the function of ideals will change: they are the non-factual anticipation of a situation which is unattainable but which already takes effect as something which can be anticipated, for it offers possibilities of leading a human life and requires the partner in the communication process to use those possibilities. Then ideals have a guiding function. But they are not imposed on one's fellow humans. Here, too, the yardstick is non-dominative communication in the sense Jesus intended.

Translated by John Griffiths

Notes

1. Cf. Bastian, *Kommunikation. Wie christliche Glaube funktionert* (Stuttgart & Berlin, 1972).

2. H.-D. Bastian, op. cit., p. 13.

3. H.-D. Bastian, op. cit., p. 14.

4. P. Watzlawick, et al., *Menschliche Kommunikation* (Berne, 1967), p. 53.

5. P. Watzlawick, op. cit., p. 51.

6. Cf. W. Schramm, *Grundfragen der Kommunikationsforschung* (Munich, 1968), pp. 9-26.

7. Cf. J. Kopperschmidt, 'Worte, nichts als Worte—Macht und Ohnmacht der Redenden', in *Theologica Practica*, 12 (1967), 1, p. 41.

8. J. Kopperschmidt, *Allgemeine Rhetorik* (Stuttgart, 1973).

9. Cf., G. Dux, 'Zum Erkenntnisfortschritt in der Soziologie', in *Zur Debatte*, 6 (1975), 5, p. 15.

10. G. Dux, op. cit., p. 16.

11. Cf. W. Loch, 'Sprache', in H. Speck & G. Wehle (eds.), *Handbuch pädagogischer Grundbegriffe*, II (Munich, 1970), p. 483.

12. K. Rahner, *Strukturwandel der Kirche als Aufgabe und Chance* (Frieburg im Breisgau, 1972), p. 77.

13. K. W. Dahm, 'Religiöse Kommunikation und kirchliche Institution', in N. Luhmann & D. Stoodt (eds.), *Religion—System und Socialisation* (Darmstadt, 1972), p. 138.

14. 'Domination' is distinguished—in the sense described by H. Marcuse in *Triebstruktur und Gesellschaft* (Frankfurt, 1971), p. 41—from the 'rational exercise of power'. Accordingly an exercise of power which emanates from human volition and is directed to the functioning of an organization, is wholly compatible with freedom from domination.

15. P. Eicher, *Solidarischer Glaube* (Düsseldorf, 1975), p. 51.

16. M. Kehl, *Kirche als Institution* (Frankfurt, 1976).

17. J. Gnilka, *Jesus Christus nach den frühen Zeugnissen des Glaubens* (Munich, 1970), p. 81.

18. J. Blank, *Das Evangelium als Guarantie der Freiheit* (Würzburg, 1970), pp. 52 ff.

19. P. Eicher, op. cit., p. 49.

20. Cf. the term 'social behaviour' or 'action' in M. Weber, *Wirtschaft und Gesellschaft* (Tübingen, 1956), p. 1, and the difference in the categorical application of 'action' or 'behaviour' and 'accession' or 'access' in J. Habermas *Theorie und Praxis* (Frankfurt, 1971), pp. 308 ff.

21. Cf. M. Kehl, op. cit., e.g., pp. 103 ff.

22. Cf. H. Peukert, op. cit., p. 310.

23. H. Peukert, op. cit., pp. 16, 283 ff.

24. P. Eicher, op. cit., p. 49.

25. L. Krappmann, *Soziologische Dimensionen der Identität* (Stuttgart, 1975).

26. L. Krappmann, op. cit., pp. 8, 9.

27. L. Krappmann, op. cit., pp. 70 ff.

28. L. Krappmann, op. cit., p. 52.

29. E. Goffmann, *Asylums* (Garden City, 1961).

30. Cf., L. Krappmann, op. cit., pp. 40 ff., 122 ff.

31. L. Krappmann, op. cit., p. 126.

32. L. Krappmann, op. cit., p. 75.

33. L. Krappmann, op. cit., p. 41.

34. H. Peukert, op. cit., p. 260.

35. J. Habermas, op. cit., p. 19.

36. P. Watzlawick, op. cit., p. 81.

37. W. Kasper, *Glaube im Wandel der Geschichte* (Mainz, 1970), p. 128.

38. R. Zerfas, 'Herrschaftsfreie Kommunikations—eine Forderung an die kirchliche Verkündigung'? in *Diakonia*, 4 (1973), p. 340.

39. S. Carmichael, 'Black Power' in D. Cooper (ed.), *Dialectic of Liberation* (London & New York, 1968).

40. J.-B. Metz, 'Theologie as Biography' in *Concilium* 12 (1976) (only available in German and French editions).

41. J.-B. Metz, loc. cit., p. 312.

42. Cf., W. Gossmann, 'The Effects of Faulty Communication' in *Concilium* 12 (1976) (only available in German and French editions).

43. Cf. H. Ernst & C. Koch, 'Warum Menschen gefühlsleer sind' in *Psychologie heute*, 4 (1977), 3, p. 13.

44. J. Bill, 'Unsere Angst vor der Berührung,' in *Pastoralblatt* 28 (1976), 9, pp. 281 ff.

45. J. Habermas, *Erkenntnis und Interesse* (Frankfurt, 1975), pp. 262 ff. (trans., *Knowledge and Human Interests,* London & Boston, 1972).

Contributors

GREGORY BAUM is professor of theology and sociology at St. Michael's College of the University of Toronto. He is editor of *The Ecumenist* and the *Journal of Ecumenical Studies,* and author of *Man Becoming* (1970), *New Horizon* (1972) and *Religion and Alienation* (1975).

WOLFGANG BARTHOLOMÄUS studied philosophy and theology at Frankfurt and education at Munich. He is professor of practical theology in the Catholic theology division of Tübingen University. He has published on catechetics, communications and religion, and education.

GIOVANNI CERETI was ordained in 1960. He is especially concerned with evangelical renewal and ecumenism. He has published on penance in the early Church and on the religious life today.

ED GRACE studied at the Catholic University of America and at the Gregorian University in Rome. He is the editor-founder of *NTC News* —an Italian-based ecumenical news agency specializing in the phenomenon of 'faith-politics'.

ANDREW GREELEY studied at St. Mary of the Lake Seminary and at the University of Chicago. He teaches in the department of sociology at the University of Chicago and is senior study director of the National Opinion Research Centre at Chicago. Among his published works are *The Hesitant Pilgrim: American Catholicism after the Council* (1966), *A Future to Hope In* (1969), and *Contemporary Religion* (1972).

RUDOLF SIEBERT studied at Mainz and Münster universities, and at the Catholic University of America in Washington. He has taught, lectured and written widely on social ethics since coming to the USA. He is professor of religions and society at Western Michigan University in Kalamazoo, Michigan.

BRIAN SMITH, SJ, studied at Fordham University, Columbia University, Woodstock College, Union Theological Seminary and Yale. Since 1976 he has been research associate in interdisciplinary research on the rôle of the Church in the promotion of social justice. He spent eleven months in field research in Chile in 1975, and has published several articles on Chile.

REYES MATE studied at the Le Saulchoir faculty in Paris and at Münster University under the direction of J. B. Metz. He is now director of the Editorial Mañana in Madrid. He has published on atheism as a political problem and on problems of sociology and Christianity in the modern age, and has collaborated with the liberation theologian Hugo Assmann.

JANICE NEWSON is associate professor and chairperson in the department of sociology at Glendon College, York University, Toronto. She has published on community studies, and the Roman Catholic clerical exodus.

ANDRÉ ROUSSEAU spent several years at the Socio-religious Research Centre of the University of Louvain, Belgium. He teaches at the Institut Catholique de Paris in the field of sociology of religion. He has researched into French Catholicism and has published several articles and books on religious institutions and attitudes.

OSMUND SCHREUDER teaches in the field of cultural and liturgical sociology in the social science faculty of the Catholic University of Nijmegen, the Netherlands. Among his publications is a collaborative work on priests and birth-control.

KENNETH WESTHUES studied at Conception College and Vanderbilt University. He has taught at Fordham University, New York, and the Universities of Guelph and Western Ontario, Canada. He is chairperson of the sociology department at the University of Waterloo, Canada. He has published on the religious community and the secular state, and on various aspects of American Catholicism.